Stress Relief Made Easy

Simple Practices for Emotional Well-Being

—

Author

LIZ SHERIDAN

This book is a work of nonfiction. The names, characters, experiences, and advice are based on the author's research, life experiences, and insights. While every effort has been made to ensure the accuracy and usefulness of the content, the author and publisher assume no responsibility for errors, omissions, or any outcomes related to the application of the information presented.

Contents

Introduction ---------- 1

Chapter 1: Box Breathing ---------- 7

Chapter 2: Take a Nature Walk ---------- 19

Chapter 3: The Healing Power of Music ---------- 29

Chapter 4: Journaling ---------- 41

Chapter 5: Sip Herbal Tea ---------- 55

Chapter 6: Warm Bath or Shower ---------- 63

Chapter 7: Progressive Muscle Relaxation ---------- 71

Chapter 8: The Role of Music & Exercise ---------- 75

Chapter 9: Gratitude List ---------- 79

Chapter 10: Do a Brain Dump ---------- 83

Chapter 11: Stretch ---------- 87

Chapter 12: Listen to Music ---------- 91

Chapter 13: Drink Water ---------- 95

Chapter 14: Eat a Snack Mindfully ---------- 99

Chapter 15: Call or Text a Friend ---------- 103

Chapter 16: Try Aromatherapy ---------- 107

Chapter 17: Name Your Emotions ---------- 111

Chapter 18: Visualization ---------- 115

Chapter 19: Do a Puzzle or Game ------------------------- 119

Chapter 20: Take a Power Nap ---------------------------- 123

Chapter 21: Repeat a Mantra ------------------------------- 127

Chapter 22: Declutter a Tiny Space ----------------------- 131

Chapter 23: Laugh -- 135

Chapter 24: Practice Saying "No" ------------------------ 139

Chapter 25: Pet an Animal --------------------------------- 143

Chapter 26: Try a Grounding Object --------------------- 147

Chapter 27: Light a Candle -------------------------------- 151

Chapter 28: Do a One-Minute Task ---------------------- 155

Conclusion: Your Journey to Lasting Well-Being ------- 159

References: Your Journey to Lasting Well-Being ------- 163

Introduction

Imagine this: It's 2pm on a sunny Tuesday, and you're sitting at your desk, feeling like your brain is a browser with forty-seven tabs open, three of them blasting odd music, and one is definitely a pop-up ad you can't close. Your shoulders are creeping toward your ears, your jaw is clenched, and that familiar knot in your stomach is making itself at home again.

Sound familiar? That is stress! Stress is as universal as that first cup of coffee in the morning. But here's the deal: while stress is inevitable, suffering through it without any tools doesn't have to be. That's why you're here reading this book, which is about to become your go-to guide to managing stress in a way that easily works for you.

Why Another Book About Stress?

It's a great question to ask, I even did the same in the course of writing this book. I get it, the self-help section and niche is overloaded with books claiming to change your life in thirty days or less, but this one is different. We're not promising to eliminate your stress altogether. Instead, we're offering you some simple and science-backed techniques you can use when life throws you a curveball.

Think of stress like the weather: you can't control when it rains, but you can keep an umbrella handy. These easy to execute techniques? They are your umbrella collection designed to help you weather the storm without getting soaked. Here is another good news: stress relief doesn't require a degree in psychology or a gym membership. In fact, some of the most effective techniques are simple things you already do, like breathing, walking, or drinking a glass of water. When you approach these with intention, they become powerful tools for calming your mind.

The Science Made Simple

Understanding what's happening in your body when you're stressed can make a huge difference in how you respond. Stress triggers your "*fight-or-flight*" response, which releases hormones like cortisol and adrenaline. These hormones increase heart rate and breathing, preparing you to deal with immediate threats, like an ancient predator chasing you. The problem is, your body doesn't differentiate between a physical threat and emotional stress. So, when you're facing a tight deadline, your body reacts the same way it would if you were face-to-face with a saber-toothed tiger.

This stress response can be helpful in short bursts, but when it becomes chronic, it negatively impacts your health. Studies show that prolonged exposure to elevated cortisol levels can lead to a variety of health problems, including anxiety, insomnia, and even heart disease (Lupien et al., 2009). Luckily, we also have a built-in counterbalance: the parasympathetic nervous system, or "*rest-and-digest*" mode. Activating this system helps you feel calm, clear-headed, and able to process emotions more effectively. All the techniques in this book are designed to stimulate the parasympathetic system, helping you turn off the stress response and regain a sense of balance.

How This Book Works (And How It Doesn't)

This book is a toolkit, not a rigid program. Feeling anxious? Try box breathing. Overwhelmed? A brain dump or decluttering might help. Disconnected? Spend time with a pet or call a friend. There's no stress-relief police here, and there's no "*right*" way to use the techniques. Some techniques will resonate with you immediately, while others might take some time to feel natural. The goal is to try, adjust, and experiment with what works best for you.

At the end of each chapter, you'll find a section to track your experience. This isn't about adding more to your to-do list; it's about observing what works and when. Tracking helps you gain insight into your personal stress patterns, like when and how different techniques work best. This self-awareness is not only a game-changer but a life saver. Research shows that people who track their habits or behaviors are more likely to stick with them and experience positive outcomes (Kohli et al., 2018). By tracking your stress relief techniques, you'll gradually build a personalized toolkit that suits your lifestyle and preferences.

In the pages ahead, you'll find many stress-relief techniques. Some are simple and take under a minute (like drinking water mindfully), while others might become your go-to practices (like evening gratitude lists or nature walks). Each technique is supported by science and designed to help you manage stress in a way that works for your body and your life. By understanding why these techniques work, you'll be able to adapt them to your specific needs and circumstances. The most powerful techniques don't require a lot of time or money, they require your attention and intention.

Your stress relief reality starts here! Remember, seeking stress relief is a sign of wisdom, not weakness. Stress is a human experience, not something to "*overcome,*" but something to manage skillfully. It's like building a muscle: the more you practice, the better you get at handling it. Some days you'll nail it, using every technique with ease. Other days, you might fall back into old patterns, and that's okay too. The goal isn't to eliminate stress, but to create a more responsive relationship with it. You have more control over your internal experience than you might think, and these tools will help you unlock that power.

You're already doing better than you think. The fact that you're here, reading this, seeking ways to manage stress with self-compassion shows incredible awareness. Your efforts to feel better are valuable. Stress is not a flaw, it's a natural part of being human. What matters is how you choose to manage it. Some days, you'll remember to use these techniques and feel great. Other days, you'll forget and end up stress-eating cookies in front of a Netflix binge. Both are part of the journey. The key is consistency and patience with yourself. It's like gardening; some seeds sprout quickly, others take time, but every effort counts. Keep showing up, keep trying, and most importantly, keep being kind to yourself along the way. Ready to start building your stress relief toolkit? Let's begin with the foundation of all calm: learning to breathe like you mean it.

How to Use Your Record Pages

Throughout this book, each technique includes guidance for tracking your experience. This isn't homework, it's detective work to help you understand what works best for you.

What to Track:

- When you tried the technique (time of day, situation)
- How you felt before and after (energy level, mood, stress level)
- What worked well and what felt challenging
- Any modifications you made to fit your needs
- Patterns you notice over time

Simple Tracking Template:

Date/Time: ____________________

Situation: (What was happening when you felt stressed?) ____________

____

Stress Level Before: 1-10 scale______________________________

Technique Used: ____

How Long: ____

Stress Level After: 1-10 scale________________________________

Notes: (What did you notice? What worked? What would you change?)

____

____

____

____

____

Will I use this again? Yes ☐ / Maybe ☐ / No ☐

Remember: The goal is awareness, not perfection. Even noting "*forgot to track but felt better*" is valuable information about your stress relief journey.

1

Box Breathing

Consider this your emergency calm button

There is something almost magical about watching a baby sleep. Their tiny chest rises and falls in perfect rhythm, completely relaxed, utterly peaceful. No tension in their shoulders, no worried furrow in their brow; just pure, effortless breathing. We all started there, breathing like champions, but somewhere along the way, many of us forgot how to do it properly.

If you've ever noticed yourself holding your breath during a tense moment, breathing shallowly when you're anxious, or taking those quick, chest-only breaths when you're stressed, you're not alone. Modern life has a way of hijacking our natural breathing patterns, turning what should be our most reliable stress-relief tool into something we barely notice we're doing wrong. But here's the beautiful thing: you can reclaim your breath. And when you do, you're not just changing how you breathe; you're literally changing how your entire nervous system responds to stress. Box breathing is like having a remote control for your anxiety, and today you're going to learn how to use it.

Why Box Breathing Works: The Science Made Simple

Let's start with a little biology lesson that will make you appreciate your body's incredible design. Your breathing is controlled by both your conscious mind (when you decide to take a deep breath) and your unconscious mind (the breathing that happens automatically while you sleep). This dual control system is actually a secret pathway to influencing your stress response.

When you're stressed, your sympathetic nervous system, which is your body's alarm system, kicks into high gear. Your breathing becomes rapid and shallow, usually happening high up in your chest rather than deep in your belly. This type of breathing actually sends a signal back to your brain saying, "*Yep, we're definitely in danger here. Keep those stress hormones coming!*"

It's like being stuck in a feedback loop where stress causes shallow breathing, which signals more stress, which causes even more shallow breathing. Not exactly helpful when you're trying to calm down.

Box breathing breaks this cycle by deliberately activating your parasympathetic nervous system, which is your body's "*rest and digest*" mode. When you breathe slowly and deeply, especially when you extend your exhale, you're sending a clear message to your brain: "*Actually, we're safe here. You can call off the alarm.*"

Research backs this up beautifully. A study published in *Frontiers in Psychology* found that just five minutes of controlled breathing exercises significantly reduced anxiety levels and improved mood in participants. Another fascinating study from Harvard Medical School showed that slow, deep breathing techniques can lower heart rate and blood pressure within minutes, literally giving your cardiovascular system a chance to relax.

What's happening inside your body during box breathing is remarkable. The controlled rhythm stimulates your vagus nerve, which runs from your brainstem down through your chest and abdomen. Think of the vagus nerve as your body's internal peacekeeping force. When researchers measured vagal tone (how well this nerve functions) in people who practiced regular breathing exercises, they found significant improvements in stress resilience and emotional regulation.

The beauty of box breathing specifically lies in its structure. The four equal parts: **inhale, hold, exhale, hold**, which create a rhythm that's both predictable and meditative. Your mind has something to focus on (counting), which helps interrupt anxious thoughts, while your body receives consistent, calming signals. Think of it like this: if your stress response is a runaway train, box breathing is both the brake and the conductor, bringing everything back under control with steady, reliable rhythm.

Why Box Breathing is a Technique That Travels Well?

Box breathing has quite the resume. Navy SEALs use it before missions to stay calm under pressure. Athletes use it to manage pre-competition nerves. Emergency room doctors use it between intense cases. Business executives use it before important presentations. And countless parents use it to avoid completely losing their minds during their toddler's public meltdowns.

The military's adoption of this technique isn't just tradition, it's based on solid evidence. Studies of tactical breathing (the military term for box breathing) show it can help maintain cognitive performance under extreme stress. When researchers tested soldiers' decision-making abilities after breathing exercises, they found significantly better focus and reduced stress hormone levels compared to control groups.

What makes box breathing so universally appealing is its simplicity and portability. You don't need any equipment, apps, or special environments. You can do it sitting in traffic, before a difficult conversation, in the bathroom during a stressful workday, or lying in bed when your mind won't stop racing at 2 AM.

The technique gets its name from the visual of a box; **four equal sides, four equal breaths**. Some people find it helpful to actually visualize drawing a box in their mind as they breathe, tracing up one side on the inhale, across the top during the first hold, down the other side on the exhale, and across the bottom during the final hold.

Step-by-Step: Your First Box Breathing Session

Let's walk through this together, as if I'm sitting right next to you. Don't worry about being perfect, there's no breathing police, and the only way to "*fail*" at box breathing is not to try it at all.

Getting Started:

First, find a comfortable position. You can sit in a chair with your feet flat on the floor, lie down on your back, or even stand if that's what's available. The key is to be comfortable enough that you won't be distracted by physical discomfort, but alert enough that you won't drift off to sleep (unless that's the goal, in which case, carry on).

Place one hand on your chest and one hand on your belly. This isn't required for the technique to work, but it helps you notice what's happening with your breathing. When you're breathing optimally, the hand on your belly should move more than the hand on your chest.

The Four-Count Rhythm:

Step 1: Inhale (4 counts)

Breathe in slowly through your nose, counting "*one, two, three, four*" at a pace that feels natural; not rushed, not dragged out. You're aiming for about one second per count, but don't stress about being exact. Allow your belly to expand like a balloon filling with air. If you notice your shoulders rising toward your ears, gently let them drop and focus on breathing "*into*" your belly instead of your chest.

Step 2: Hold (4 counts)

Retain the breath comfortably for four counts. This isn't a contest to see how long you can hold your breath, it should feel sustainable and calm. If four counts feels too long, try three counts instead. If it feels too short, you can work up to five or six counts over time. The goal is rhythm, not endurance.

Step 3: Exhale (4 counts)

Release the breath slowly through your mouth, again counting to four. Some people prefer to exhale through their nose, which is fine too; do whatever feels more natural. Let your belly gently fall as the air leaves your lungs. This exhale is where the magic happens, it's the part that most directly signals your nervous system to relax.

Step 4: Hold Empty (4 counts)

After you've exhaled, pause for four counts before beginning the next inhale. This might feel a bit unusual at first, as we don't typically hold our breath when our lungs are empty, but it's an important part of the rhythm. This pause helps reset your breathing pattern and completes the "*box.*"

Repeat the Cycle:

Continue this pattern for at least four complete cycles, though you can do it for as long as feels good. Most people find that **4-8** cycles are enough to feel a noticeable shift in their stress level, but some enjoy continuing for several minutes.

When to Use Box Breathing

The wonderful thing about having box breathing in your toolkit is its versatility. Research shows that breathing techniques are most effective when used consistently, both as preventive tools and in response to acute stress. Here are some situations where it can be particularly helpful:

1. **Before stressful events:** Use it in the parking lot before a job interview, in the waiting room before a medical appointment, or in your car before walking into a difficult meeting.

2. **During acute stress:** When you notice your heart racing, your thoughts spiraling, or your body tensing up, box breathing can help interrupt the stress response in real-time. Studies show that controlled breathing can reduce cortisol levels; your primary stress hormone, within minutes of practice.

3. **For better sleep:** Many people find that doing several cycles of box breathing while lying in bed helps quiet their mind and prepare their body for rest. Sleep researchers have found that breathing exercises can improve sleep quality by activating the same relaxation response that naturally occurs as we drift off.

4. **As a daily practice:** Some people incorporate box breathing into their morning routine to start the day with calm focus, or into their evening routine to help transition from work mode to relaxation mode.

5. **In response to anger or frustration:** When you feel your temper rising, box breathing can help you pause and respond rather than react. It's like giving yourself a moment to choose your response rather than being hijacked by your emotions.

Building Your Box Breathing Practice

Like any skill, box breathing gets easier and more effective with practice. Research on habit formation suggests that it takes about 21 days to establish a new routine, but the benefits of breathing exercises can often be felt much sooner. Don't worry about being perfect from day one, even experienced practitioners sometimes find their minds wandering or their rhythm off. The key is consistency, not perfection.

Some people like to set a daily reminder on their phone to practice box breathing, while others prefer to use it as needed when stress arises. Both approaches work well. What matters most is that you actually use the technique rather than just knowing about it.

You might find it helpful to practice when you're already calm at first, so you're familiar with the technique when you really need it. It's like learning to use a fire extinguisher, you want to know how it works before there's actually a fire.

Consider starting with just one or two sessions per day. Maybe try it with your morning coffee or tea, creating a small ritual of calm before your day begins. Or use it as a transition between work and home, helping you shift gears mentally and emotionally.

The Ripple Effects of Box Breathing

What's fascinating about box breathing is that its benefits extend far beyond the minutes you spend actually doing it. A longitudinal study published in the *Journal of Clinical Medicine* followed people who practiced breathing exercises for eight weeks and found improvements not only in stress levels but also in immune function, blood pressure, and overall quality of life.

Regular practice can improve your overall stress resilience, help you sleep better, improve your focus, and even lower your blood pressure over time.

Many people find that after practicing box breathing regularly, they naturally start breathing more deeply throughout the day. They notice when their breathing becomes shallow during stress and can adjust it without even thinking about it. It's like developing a sixth sense for your own stress levels.

You might also notice that you become more aware of your body's stress signals in general. That tension in your shoulders, the tightness in your jaw, the way your stomach clenches during difficult conversations; all of these become information you can use to take better care of yourself.

Neuroscience research shows that regular breathing practice actually changes brain structure over time, strengthening areas associated with attention and emotional regulation while reducing activity in the amygdala; your brain's alarm center. It's like upgrading your internal stress management system.

Making Box Breathing Your Own

While the basic **4-4-4-4** pattern is a great starting point, feel free to adapt box breathing to fit your needs and preferences. These are some variations you can try:

1. **Visual box breathing:** As you breathe, imagine drawing a box in your mind, or actually trace a box on your leg with your finger as you follow the pattern.

2. **Counted box breathing:** Instead of just counting to four, try counting "**in-2-3-4, hold-2-3-4, out-2-3-4, hold-2-3-4.**" Some people find the rhythm of words more engaging than numbers.

3. **Color breathing:** Imagine breathing in a calming color (like blue or green) and breathing out a stress color (like red or gray). This adds a visualization component that some people find helpful.

4. **Nature box breathing:** If you're outside, try syncing your breathing with natural rhythms; the gentle sway of trees, the rhythm of waves, or the steady chirping of birds.

The most important thing is finding a version that feels sustainable and helpful for you. Box breathing should feel like a gift you give yourself, not another item on your to-do list. Your breathing success story starts now. As you begin incorporating box breathing into your life, remember that you're not just learning a technique, you're reclaiming one of your most fundamental tools for self-care. Every time you choose to breathe consciously instead of letting stress control your breathing, you're taking back a little bit of control over your internal experience.

Some days, box breathing will feel like a miracle cure, instantly shifting you from stressed to calm. Other days, it might feel like you're just going through the motions, and that's okay too. The benefits are cumulative, building over time like interest in a savings account.

Be patient with yourself as you learn. If you forget to use box breathing during a stressful moment, don't add self-criticism to your stress. Simply remember for next time. If you find your mind wandering during the technique, gently bring it back without judgment. Every moment of conscious breathing is a victory worth celebrating.

Your breath has been with you since the moment you were born, and it will be with you until your last day. Learning to use it skillfully is one of the most practical gifts you can give yourself. You now have a tool that's always available, completely free, and more powerful than you might imagine.

Take a moment right now to try one cycle of box breathing. Inhale for four, hold for four, exhale for four, hold for four. Notice how you feel. That's the beginning of your box breathing journey; simple, accessible, and surprisingly powerful. Cheers to your new superpower. Use it wisely, use it often, and most importantly, use it with kindness toward yourself.

Tracking Your Box Breathing Practice

What to Notice:

- Your stress level before and after (**1-10 scale**)
- How the counting felt (easy, challenging, just right)
- Any physical sensations you noticed
- Whether your mind wandered and how you handled it
- The best times of day for your practice
- Situations where box breathing was most/least helpful

Box Breathing Practice Log:

Date: ________ **Time:** ________ **Location:** ________________

Duration: ________________

Stress Level Before: 1-10

Stress Level After: 1-10

Count that felt right: 3-3-3-3 / 4-4-4-4 / 5-5-5-5 / Other: _____________

What I noticed: ☐ Mind wandered a lot ☐ Felt physically calmer ☐ Breathing felt more natural ☐ Hard to focus on counting ☐ Felt sleepy/ relaxed ☐ Wanted to continue longer

Best part of this session: ____________________________________

____

____

What I'd change next time: __________________________________

Will I use this technique again? Definitely / Maybe / Probably not

Weekly Reflection:

After practicing for a week, what patterns do you notice? When is box breathing most helpful for you? What adjustments have you made to make it work better?

2

Take a Nature Walk

Your Daily Dose of Earth Medicine

There's something almost comical about how we've complicated the simple act of walking outside. We track our steps, optimize our routes, calculate our calories burned, and listen to podcasts about productivity while we're supposed to be relaxing. Meanwhile, our ancestors just walked. They stepped outside their caves or huts, looked around at the world, and let their feet carry them wherever they needed to go.

Somewhere along the way, we forgot that walking in nature isn't just exercise, it's medicine. Not the kind that comes in a bottle with a list of side effects, but the kind that's been freely available to humans for millennia. The kind that works on your body, mind, and spirit all at once, without requiring a prescription or a copay.

If you've ever felt your shoulders drop and your breathing deepen the moment you step outside, you've experienced this medicine firsthand. If you've ever noticed that your biggest problems seem more manageable after a walk around the block, you've tapped into something profound. Today, we're going to explore how to use nature walks as a reliable stress-relief tool, turning a simple stroll into a powerful reset button for your nervous system.

The Science of Stepping Outside

Let's start with what happens in your body when you trade indoor air for the great outdoors. The moment you step outside, especially into a natural environment, your body begins a fascinating cascade of positive changes that scientists are still discovering and marveling at.

First, there's the obvious benefit of movement. When you walk, your body releases endorphins, those feel-good chemicals that act like natural painkillers and mood elevators. Your heart rate increases just enough to improve circulation, sending oxygen-rich blood to your brain and muscles. This gentle cardiovascular activity helps metabolize stress hormones like cortisol and adrenaline, literally walking them out of your system.

Here is where it gets really interesting: it's not just the movement that helps—it's specifically movement in nature. Japanese researchers have extensively studied something called "*forest bathing*" or "*shinrin-yoku,*" which is essentially the practice of mindfully spending time in nature. They've found that even a 20-minute walk in a natural setting can significantly lower cortisol levels, reduce blood pressure, and boost immune function.

The secret lies in what trees and plants naturally release into the air: organic compounds called phytoncides. These airborne chemicals, which plants emit to protect themselves from insects and bacteria, actually boost our immune systems when we breathe them in. It's like nature's way of giving us a gentle health upgrade just for showing up.

Then there's the visual aspect. Our brains are wired to find natural patterns and colors soothing. The soft, irregular shapes of clouds, the gentle sway of grass, the complex patterns of tree bark; all of these give our minds a break from the harsh lines, bright screens, and artificial lighting we're exposed to indoors. This visual rest is particularly important for our overstimulated modern brains.

Natural light exposure also helps regulate your circadian rhythms, improving sleep quality and mood. Even on cloudy days, outdoor light is significantly brighter than indoor lighting, signaling to your brain that it's time to be alert and present.

The Mental Health Magic of Nature Walk

Perhaps the most profound benefits of nature walks happen in your mind. When you're walking in nature, several powerful psychological processes kick in simultaneously.

First, there's what researchers call "*soft fascination." Unlike the "hard fascination*" required by screens, traffic, or complex tasks, nature captures your attention gently. A bird singing, leaves rustling, water flowing; these naturally draw your focus without depleting your mental energy. This gives your prefrontal cortex, the part of your brain responsible for executive function and decision-making, a chance to rest and restore.

This mental rest is crucial because most of us are running on cognitive overload most of the time. We're constantly making decisions, processing information, and managing multiple streams of input. Nature walks provide what psychologists call "*cognitive restoration,*" a chance for your brain to recover from this constant stimulation.

There's also the phenomenon of "*present-moment awareness*" that naturally occurs during nature walks. When you're focused on where you're stepping, noticing the sounds around you, or observing the changing light, you're practicing a form of moving meditation. This present-moment focus interrupts the rumination and worry that often fuel our stress.

Many people find that their best insights and creative solutions come during nature walks. This isn't coincidence, it's neuroscience. When your brain isn't actively focused on a problem, it continues working on it in the background through what's called the "*default mode network.*" The gentle, rhythmic movement of walking, combined with the restorative environment of nature, creates optimal conditions for this background processing to happen.

Redefining "Nature" To Suit Your Life

Now, before you start thinking you need to live near a pristine wilderness to get these benefits, let's talk about what "*nature*" actually means for most of us. You don't need towering redwoods or mountain vistas to tap into nature's stress-relieving power. Even small doses of green space can make a significant difference.

A tree-lined street, a neighborhood park, a courtyard with some plants, or even a single tree you can sit under all count as nature. Studies have shown that even looking at nature through a window can reduce stress and improve focus. The key is getting away from the completely artificial environment of indoor spaces and connecting with living, growing things.

Urban nature walks might look different from rural ones, but they're equally valuable. That little patch of grass between sidewalks, the weeds growing through cracks in the pavement, the sky visible between buildings; all of these can serve as anchors for your attention and sources of restoration.

If you live in a highly urban area, consider seeking out whatever green spaces exist: rooftop gardens, community gardens, tree-lined streets, or even indoor spaces with lots of plants. Some cities have "*pocket parks*" or small green spaces tucked between buildings that can provide a surprising amount of natural restoration.

Step-by-Step: Your Nature Walk Practice

Let's walk through how to turn a simple walk outside into a powerful stress-relief practice. The beauty of nature walks is their simplicity, but a little intention can amplify their benefits significantly.

Preparation: The Art of Leaving Things Behind

The first step in a therapeutic nature walk actually happens before you step outside: deciding what to leave behind. This includes your phone (or at least putting it on silent and in your pocket), your to-do list, and your problem-solving mind.

I know leaving your phone behind might feel like suggesting you leave your oxygen tank at home. But here is the thing: your phone is designed to capture and fragment your attention, which is the opposite of what you're trying to achieve. Every notification, every urge to check messages or take photos, pulls you out of the present moment and back into the digital world you're trying to escape.

If you must bring your phone for safety reasons, put it on airplane mode or at least turn off notifications. Resist the urge to document every pretty flower or interesting cloud. Instead, practice the lost art of experiencing something without immediately sharing it.

Starting Out: The Transition Ritual

Before you begin walking, take a moment to consciously transition from indoor mode to outdoor mode. Stand still for a moment and take three deep breaths. Notice the temperature of the air on your skin, any sounds you can hear, the quality of light around you. This simple pause helps signal to your brain that you're shifting into a different kind of awareness.

Set an intention for your walk. It doesn't have to be profound, something simple like "*I'm going to notice what's around me*" or "*I'm going to let my mind rest*" is perfect. This intention acts like a gentle anchor, helping you remember your purpose when your mind inevitably starts wandering back to your usual concerns.

The Walk Itself: Engaging Your Senses

1. Start walking at whatever pace feels natural. This isn't a fitness walk or a race to a destination, it's a moving meditation. Leave your phone behind (or turn on airplane mode). Let your pace be relaxed and unhurried. If you find yourself rushing, consciously slow down.

2. Begin by noticing what you can see. Look up at the sky, down at the ground, and around at eye level. Notice colors, shapes, patterns, and movement. You don't need to identify or analyze everything you see, just let your eyes rest on whatever catches your attention. If you see a squirrel, wave and say hi. No one's judging.

3. Expand your awareness to sounds. What can you hear? Birds, wind, traffic, your own footsteps? Don't judge the sounds as good or bad, just notice them. Urban sounds like traffic or construction can be just as grounding as natural sounds if you approach them with curiosity rather than annoyance. Walk slowly. Look around. Notice birds, bugs, clouds, squirrels.

4. Bring in your sense of touch. Feel the air on your skin. Is it warm, cool, humid, dry? Notice the sensation of your feet touching the ground with each step. If it's safe to do so, you might touch the bark of a tree, the leaves of a plant, or feel grass under your feet.

5. Don't forget about smell. Natural environments often have subtle scents that we miss when we're rushing: the smell of earth after rain, the fragrance of flowers, the fresh scent of growing things. These scents can be deeply calming and grounding. Take deep breaths and let your thoughts wander gently.

Adapting Nature Walks to Your Life

One of the beautiful things about nature walks is how adaptable they are to different schedules, physical abilities, and environments. Let's explore how to make this practice work for your real life.

Time Variations:

- **The 5-minute reset:** Even a brief step outside and around the block can help interrupt stress and provide a mental break.
- **The 15-minute refresh:** A quarter-hour nature walk can provide significant stress relief and mental clarity.
- **The 30-minute restoration:** Half an hour in nature can create profound shifts in mood and perspective.
- **The hour-long retreat:** For times when you need deeper restoration, a longer nature walk can feel like a mini-vacation.

Physical Adaptations:

Nature walks are for every body. If walking is challenging, consider:

- Sitting outside in a natural setting and letting your senses engage with the environment
- Moving at whatever pace feels comfortable, even if it's very slow
- Using mobility aids as needed; the stress-relief benefits don't depend on speed or distance
- Choosing accessible routes like paved paths in parks or gentle trails

Weather Considerations:

Different weather conditions offer different experiences and benefits:

- **Sunny days:** Provide vitamin D and bright light exposure that can boost mood
- **Rainy days:** Offer the soothing sounds of rain and the fresh scent of wet earth (with appropriate rain gear)
- **Cloudy days:** Can feel peaceful and contemplative, with softer

light that's easy on the eyes

- **Windy days:** Provide the invigorating sensation of moving air and the sound of wind through trees

The key is dressing appropriately and adjusting expectations. A winter walk in the snow offers different pleasures than a summer evening stroll, but both can be restorative. As you begin incorporating nature walks into your stress-relief toolkit, remember that you're engaging in one of humanity's oldest healing practices. Long before we had therapists' offices and meditation apps, we had the simple wisdom of walking outside when life felt overwhelming.

Your nature walks don't need to look like anyone else's. Maybe your practice is a daily walk around your neighborhood, noticing the same trees through different seasons. Maybe it's weekend hikes in more wild places. Maybe it's sitting outside your apartment building, watching clouds and feeling the breeze.

What matters is that you're regularly giving yourself the gift of stepping outside the human-made world and reconnecting with something larger than your immediate concerns. You're practicing the radical act of being present in a world that profits from your distraction.

Every time you choose to step outside instead of scrolling through your phone, you're voting for your own well-being. Every time you pause to really look at a tree or listen to birdsong, you're practicing a form of meditation that your ancestors would recognize and approve of.

The path is literally at your feet. The medicine is as close as your nearest door. Your prescription is simple: step outside, look around, and let the earth work its quiet magic on your stressed and weary spirit. The world is waiting for you. Your next dose of earth medicine is just a walk away.

Tracking Your Nature Walking Practice

What to Notice:

- How you felt before and after your walk (energy, mood, stress level)
- What you observed in nature (seasonal changes, wildlife, weather)
- How your mind felt during the walk (calm, scattered, focused)
- Physical sensations and changes in your body
- Any insights or creative thoughts that arose
- The most restorative part of your walk

Nature Walk Log:

Date: _________ **Time:** _________ **Duration:** _________ **Location:** __ _______________________________ **Weather:** ___________________ ______________

Before the walk: Stress Level: 1-10

Energy Level: 1-10

Mood: ______________________

After the walk: Stress Level: 1-10

Energy Level: 1-10

Mood: _____________________

What I noticed in nature: ☐ Birds or other wildlife ☐ Changing seasons ☐ Interesting plants or trees ☐ Sky and clouds ☐ Sounds of nature ☐ Scents and smells ☐ Other: ____________________________________ ____________________________________

How my mind felt: ☐ Calmer than when I started ☐ More focused and clear ☐ Creative thoughts arose ☐ Worried less about problems ☐ Present and engaged ☐ Scattered but peaceful

Most memorable moment: ________________________________

What drew my attention most: ________________________________

How I'll remember this walk: ________________________________

Weekly Reflection: What patterns do you notice in your nature walking practice? What types of natural settings feel most restorative to you? How has regular time outdoors affected your overall stress levels and well-being?

3

The Healing Power of Music

We live in a world of noise. Not just the obvious kind; the traffic, construction, and endless notifications, but the subtler soundtrack of modern stress: the hum of fluorescent lights, the whir of air conditioning, the constant background chatter of televisions in waiting rooms. Our ancestors knew silence, knew the natural rhythms of wind through trees and water over stones. They understood that sound could heal as much as it could harm.

Somewhere in our rush toward progress, we forgot that music isn't just entertainment, it's medicine. The kind that doesn't require a prescription, has no side effects, and has been available to every human culture throughout history. The kind that can shift your entire nervous system in the span of a single song. Yet here we are, stressed and overwhelmed, carrying powerful sound-healing devices in our pockets while using them primarily to add more noise to our already overstimulated lives. We listen to podcasts that make us think harder, music that amps us up, or news that makes us more anxious. We've forgotten the radical act of choosing sounds that actually serve our well-being.

If you've ever felt your breathing slow when you heard a particularly beautiful piece of music, or noticed how certain songs can instantly transport you to a calmer state of mind, you've experienced the therapeutic power of sound. If you've ever put on headphones to escape the chaos around you, you've instinctively reached for one of humanity's oldest healing tools. Today, we're going to explore how to use this tool intentionally, turning the simple act of listening into a reliable path to inner peace.

The Neuroscience of Musical Medicine

When you press play on a piece of calming music, something remarkable happens in your brain, many neurochemical changes, and that is something scientists are still discovering and mapping. It's not just that you "*feel*" different when you listen to music; you literally become different, at least temporarily, on a cellular level.

Within the first few seconds of listening, your brain begins releasing a cocktail of beneficial chemicals. Dopamine, the neurotransmitter associated with pleasure and reward, starts flowing. At the same time, levels of cortisol "*your body's primary stress hormone*" begin to drop. It's as if your nervous system is receiving a gentle chemical massage from the inside out.

Dr. Suzanne Hanser's groundbreaking research at Berklee College of Music has shown that listening to music can reduce cortisol levels by up to 25% in just 30 minutes. But perhaps more outstanding, these changes begin almost immediately. Within two minutes of listening to calming music, measurable changes occur in heart rate, blood pressure, and breathing patterns.

The mechanism behind this is something called "*neuroplasticity,*" your brain's ability to form new neural pathways based on experience. When you regularly listen to calming music, you're literally rewiring your brain to access peaceful states more easily. It's like creating well-worn paths through a forest; the more you travel them, the easier they become to navigate. But there's another layer of healing happening that's even more fascinating: something called "*entrainment.*" This is your body's natural tendency to synchronize with external rhythms.

When you listen to music with a slower tempo, typically around **60 to 80**

beats per minute; your heart rate, breathing, and even brainwaves gradually slow down to match it. Your body is essentially learning to be calm by following the music's example. This entrainment effect is why lullabies work so effectively, why certain types of music can make you feel sleepy, and why the right playlist can shift your entire mood. Your nervous system is constantly listening for cues about how to respond, and music provides some of the clearest, most direct cues available.

The Frequency of Healing

Different types of music affect us in different ways, and understanding these differences can help you choose sounds that serve your specific needs. It's not just about personal preference, though that certainly matters, but about how different frequencies, rhythms, and structures interact with your nervous system.

Lower frequencies, like those found in cello music, Tibetan singing bowls, or even the deep rumble of distant thunder, tend to activate your parasympathetic nervous system; the "*rest and digest*" response that counteracts stress. These sounds seem to resonate with your body's natural rhythms, creating a sense of groundedness and stability.

Higher frequencies, like those in flute music or wind chimes, can feel uplifting and expansive, but they can also be overstimulating if you're already feeling anxious. The key is learning to read your own nervous system's responses and choose accordingly.

Instrumental music often works better for stress relief than music with lyrics because your brain doesn't have to work to process language. Without words to interpret, your mind can simply receive the music rather than analyze it. This is why you might find that songs you love and know well can sometimes be less effective for relaxation than unfamiliar instrumental pieces, since your brain wants to sing along or anticipate the next line rather than simply rest.

The concept of "*musical consonance*" also plays a role. Harmonious intervals and predictable chord progressions tend to feel more soothing than dissonant or unexpected musical elements. This doesn't mean you need to stick to simple, boring music, but rather that music with clear harmonic structure often works better for stress relief than experimental or highly complex compositions.

Repetitive patterns can be particularly calming for anxious minds. The gentle repetition of a piano arpeggio, the cyclical nature of ambient electronic music, or the rhythmic patterns of rain or ocean sounds give your nervous system something predictable to follow. In a world full of uncertainty, this predictability can be deeply soothing.

Creating Your Personal Sound Pharmacy

Think of building your calming music collection like stocking a well-equipped medicine cabinet. Just as you might keep different remedies for different ailments, you'll want different types of music for different emotional states and situations. The goal is to have a range of options that can meet you wherever you are and gently guide you toward where you want to be. Thus:

For Acute Stress Relief:

When you're feeling overwhelmed and need immediate support, look for music with very simple, repetitive structures. Think of gentle piano pieces with minimal variation, ambient electronic music with long, sustained tones, or nature sounds with subtle musical elements. The composer Max Richter's "*Sleep*" collection was specifically designed for this purpose, as was Brian Eno's "*Music for Airports*" series. These pieces don't demand your attention but provide a sonic environment that naturally calms your nervous system.

For Anxiety and Racing Thoughts:

When your mind is spinning, you need music that can help ground you without being so stimulating that it adds to the mental chatter. Classical pieces with clear, predictable structures work well; think Bach's "*Goldberg Variations*" or Pachelbel's "*Canon in D.*" The mathematical precision of these compositions can help create order in mental chaos. Acoustic guitar music, particularly fingerstyle pieces, can also be wonderfully grounding.

For Emotional Processing:

Sometimes you need music that can hold space for difficult emotions while gradually guiding you toward resolution. This might include more complex pieces that have emotional depth but ultimately resolve into peaceful places. Ludovico Einaudi's piano compositions, Ólafur Arnalds' ambient classical works, or even carefully chosen film scores can provide this kind of emotional journey.

For Sleep Preparation:

Music for sleep should be different from music for daytime relaxation. You want pieces that literally slow down over time, helping your body follow suit. Look for music that starts around 60-70 beats per minute and gradually decreases, with volumes that fade rather than remain constant. Marconi Union's "*Weightless*" was scientifically designed to reduce anxiety and promote sleep, decreasing heart rate, blood pressure, and stress hormones.

For Transition Times:

Some of the most effective uses of calming music are during transitions—between work and home, between active time and rest, or between different activities throughout the day. For these moments, you might choose music that serves as a bridge, helping you consciously shift gears rather than carrying stress from one environment to another.

The Rhythms of Musical Healing

Just as your stress levels change throughout the day, week, and seasons, your musical needs will also shift. Learning to recognize these rhythms can help you choose music that truly serves you in each moment.

Morning Music:

The music that helps you start your day might be different from what helps you wind down. Some people need gentle, uplifting music that helps them transition from sleep to wakefulness. Others benefit from slightly more energizing music that still maintains a sense of calm. Pay attention to what helps you feel centered and grounded as you begin your day.

Workday Transitions:

The music you choose during lunch breaks or between meetings can significantly impact your stress levels. Even five minutes of calming music can help reset your nervous system and improve your focus for the rest of the day. Many people find that having a specific "*reset playlist*" helps them transition more consciously between different parts of their day.

Evening Wind-Down:

Music for the evening should generally be slower and softer than daytime music, helping your body begin its natural transition toward rest. This is a good time for music that decreases in tempo and volume, gently guiding your nervous system toward sleep.

Seasonal Shifts:

Your musical preferences might change with the seasons, just as your mood and energy levels do. Winter might call for more grounding, warming music, while spring might feel better with lighter, more hopeful selections. Pay attention to these natural shifts and adjust your musical choices accordingly.

Stress-Level Matching:

Sometimes you need music that meets you where you are before it can take you where you want to go. If you're feeling highly anxious, jumping straight to very slow, meditative music might feel jarring. You might start with something slightly more active or complex, then gradually transition to gentler pieces as your nervous system settles.

Building Your Musical Wellness Practice Step-by Step

Like any stress-relief technique, using music therapeutically becomes more effective with regular practice. But unlike some other techniques, this one comes with built-in rewards that make it easier to maintain. Most people find that once they start using music intentionally for stress relief, they naturally want to continue because of how much better it makes them feel.

1. **Start Small and Consistent:** Begin with just 10-15 minutes of intentional musical listening per day. This might be during your morning coffee, your lunch break, or as part of your evening routine. Consistency is more important than duration, especially in the beginning.

2. **Create Musical Rituals:** Consider pairing calming music with other activities that support your well-being. This might be listening to gentle music while taking a bath, playing soft instrumental music during meal preparation, or using music as part of your bedtime routine. These combinations help your brain create stronger associations between the music and the feeling of calm.

3. **Experiment with Different Genres:** Don't limit yourself to what you think should be relaxing. Some people find deep peace in ambient electronic music, while others prefer classical piano or acoustic guitar. Some respond well to nature sounds, while others prefer pure instrumental mu-

sic. Your preferences might even change over time, so stay curious and open to what serves you.

4. **Notice Your Responses:** Keep a simple mental note of how different types of music affect you. Which pieces help you feel more grounded? Which ones help you transition between activities? Which ones support better sleep? This awareness will help you build a more effective personal collection over time.

5. **Expand Gradually:** As you become more comfortable with the practice, you might experiment with longer sessions, different types of music, or using music to support specific goals like creative work or emotional processing.

Your Personal Sound Prescription

As you begin incorporating calming music into your daily life, remember that you're engaging with one of humanity's oldest and most universal healing practices. Every culture throughout history has recognized music's power to heal, comfort, and restore. You're not just listening to music, you're participating in an ancient tradition of using sound as medicine.

Your musical needs will be unique to you, shaped by your personal history, cultural background, and individual nervous system. The lullabies you heard as a child, the music that played during peaceful moments in your life, the sounds of nature that remind you of places you've felt safe, all of these create neural pathways that can be activated for healing.

Trust your body's wisdom more than your mind's preferences. You might be someone who finds deep peace in music you never thought you'd enjoy, or someone who discovers that familiar songs work better for you than unfamiliar ones. There's no wrong way to use music for healing, only different ways that work for different people.

Start where you are, with whatever music feels appealing to you right now. Pay attention to how different sounds affect your breathing, your muscle tension, your thoughts, and your overall sense of well-being. Let your experience be your guide. Every time you choose to fill your environment with peaceful sounds rather than chaotic ones, you're voting for your own well-being. Every time you use music to consciously shift your emotional state, you're practicing a form of self-care that your nervous system will thank you for.

The healing power of music is always available to you. It doesn't require special equipment, expensive treatments, or perfect conditions. It only requires your willingness to listen; not just with your ears, but with your whole being. Your personal sound haven is as close as your nearest speaker or headphones. Your prescription for musical medicine is as simple as pressing play and allowing the sounds to work their gentle magic on your stressed and weary spirit. The music is waiting for you. Your next dose of sound healing is just a song away.

Tracking Your Musical Healing Practice

What to Notice:

- How you felt before and after listening (stress level, mood, energy)
- Physical changes in your body (breathing, muscle tension, heart rate)
- What types of music work best for different situations
- How music affects your sleep quality
- Any emotions or memories that arise during listening
- Which pieces feel most restorative to you

Musical Wellness Log:

Date: _________ **Time:** _________ **Duration:** _________

Music/Artist: _________________________________

Setting: ☐ Home ☐ Work ☐ Commute ☐ Outdoors ☐ Other:_______

Purpose: ☐ Stress relief ☐ Sleep preparation ☐ Transition between activities ☐ Emotional processing ☐ Background calm ☐ Other: ______

Before listening:

Stress Level (1-10): _____________

Energy Level (1-10): ____________

Mood: ________________________

Physical tension areas: ______________________________________

After listening:

Stress Level (1-10): _____

Energy Level (1-10): _____

Mood: ______________

Physical changes noticed: ______________

What I noticed during listening: ☐Breathing became slower/deeper ☐ Muscles relaxed ☐ Mind became quieter ☐ Felt more present ☐ Emotions arose ☐ Felt transported or peaceful ☐ Other: ______________

Effectiveness for intended purpose: ☐ Very helpful ☐ Somewhat helpful ☐ Neutral ☐ Not helpful

Would I listen to this again in similar circumstances? ☐ Definitely ☐ Probably ☐ Maybe ☐ Probably not

Most peaceful moment: ____________________________________

What I want to remember about this experience: ________________

____

Weekly Reflection: What patterns do you notice in your musical preferences? Which types of music consistently help you feel calmer? How has regular musical stress relief affected your overall well-being? What combinations of music and activities work best for you?

4

Journaling

The Art of Meeting Yourself on Paper

We've become a culture obsessed with communication; texting, posting, commenting, sharing every thought that crosses our minds with the digital world. We document our meals, our moods, our mundane daily activities for audiences of friends and strangers. Yet somehow, in all this external expression, we've lost touch with the most important conversation of all: **the one we have with ourselves**.

Our ancestors understood something we've forgotten. They wrote letters to themselves, kept diaries, recorded their inner worlds with the same care they used to document their outer ones. They knew that thoughts and feelings, left unexamined, have a way of growing wild and unwieldy, like gardens left untended. They understood that writing wasn't just a way to remember, it was a way to heal.

Somewhere along the way, journaling became associated with teenage angst or literary pretension. We started thinking we needed to be "*good writers*" to benefit from putting pen to paper, or that our thoughts weren't interesting enough to be worth recording. We forgot that journaling isn't about creating beautiful prose or profound insights, it's about creating space for our inner experience to breathe.

If you've ever felt clearer after venting to a friend, or experienced relief after writing a long email (even if you never sent it), you've tasted the medicine that journaling offers. If you've ever had a breakthrough while explaining a problem out loud, you understand the power of giving voice to your inner world. Today, we're going to explore how to harness this power intentionally, turning the simple act of writing into a reliable tool for emotional clarity and mental peace.

The Neuroscience of Narrative Healing

When you sit down with a blank page and begin to write about your experiences, something therapeutic happens in your brain. You're not just recording thoughts, you're literally rewiring your neural networks, creating new pathways for understanding and processing your life.

Dr. James Pennebaker's groundbreaking research at the University of Texas has revealed that expressive writing, the kind where you explore your deepest thoughts and feelings about difficult experiences, can have profound effects on both mental and physical health. People who engage in regular expressive writing show improved immune function, lower blood pressure, reduced symptoms of depression and anxiety, and even better sleep quality.

The mechanism behind this healing lies in what neuroscientists call "*affect labeling,*" the process of putting emotions into words. When you're experiencing strong emotions, your amygdala (the brain's alarm center) can become hyperactivated, flooding your system with stress hormones and making it difficult to think clearly. The act of writing about these emotions activates your prefrontal cortex, the brain region responsible for executive function and emotional regulation.

This isn't just metaphorical, brain imaging studies show that when people write about emotional experiences, activity in the amygdala decreases while activity in the prefrontal cortex increases. You're literally shifting your brain from a state of emotional reactivity to one of thoughtful reflection. It's like giving your nervous system a chance to catch its breath and reorganize itself.

There is another layer of healing happening through what psychologists call "*narrative coherence.*" When you write about your experiences, you're creating a story that makes sense of what might otherwise feel like random, overwhelming events. This process of meaning-making is fundamental to psychological well-being. Humans are story-telling creatures, and we need our lives to feel like coherent narratives rather than collections of disconnected experiences.

The act of translating internal experience into written language also engages both hemispheres of your brain. Your right brain, which processes emotions and experiences holistically, works with your left brain, which specializes in language and linear thinking. This integration can lead to insights and understanding that wouldn't be available through either emotional processing or logical analysis alone.

The Alchemy of Emotional Expression

There is something almost magical about the moment when a feeling that's been swirling chaotically in your mind suddenly becomes clear on paper. What felt overwhelming and shapeless in your head transforms into something manageable and specific when you give it words. This transformation is the heart of journaling's healing power.

Unexpressed emotions don't simply disappear, they accumulate in our bodies and minds like sediment in a river, creating blockages and disturbances in our natural flow. When we carry unprocessed feelings, they influence our thoughts, decisions, and reactions in ways we often don't recognize. That irritability that seems to come from nowhere, the anxiety that feels disproportionate to the situation, the sadness that colors everything; these can all be manifestations of emotional material that needs expression and integration.

Writing provides a safe container for these feelings. Unlike verbal expression, which happens in real-time and can feel pressured or performative, writing allows you to explore emotions at your own pace, without judgment or the need to make sense to anyone else. You can be messy, contradictory, or raw in ways that might feel too vulnerable in spoken conversation.

The page becomes a trusted confidant, someone who listens without interrupting, judges without criticizing, and holds space for whatever needs to be expressed. This unconditional acceptance can be profoundly healing, especially for people who struggle to express difficult emotions in their relationships or who have learned to suppress their feelings as a survival strategy.

Research has shown that the benefits of expressive writing don't require literary skill or even grammatical correctness. What matters is the willingness to be honest and the commitment to exploring your inner landscape with curiosity rather than judgment. Your journal doesn't care about typos, run-on sentences, or whether your thoughts are "*interesting enough.*" It simply provides space for your authentic experience.

Type of Journaling for Inner Discovery

Different types of journaling serve different purposes, like different rooms in a house that support different activities. Understanding these variations can help you choose the approach that best serves your current needs and circumstances.

1. **Stream-of-Consciousness Writing:**

This is perhaps the most foundational form of therapeutic journaling. You simply write whatever comes to mind, without censoring, editing, or trying to make sense. Set a timer for 10-20 minutes and let your hand move across the page, following whatever thoughts arise. This practice, sometimes called "*morning pages*" after Julia Cameron's work in "*The Artist's Way,*" helps clear mental clutter and often reveals insights that surprise you.

The key to stream-of-consciousness writing is maintaining forward momentum. Don't stop to correct spelling, don't worry about coherence, and don't judge what's emerging. If you get stuck, write "*I don't know what to write*" until something else comes. This practice helps bypass your internal critic and accesses deeper layers of awareness.

2. **Emotional Processing Journaling:**

When you're dealing with specific difficult emotions or situations, focused emotional writing can be incredibly powerful. Choose a situation that's causing you stress and write about it continuously for 15-20 minutes, exploring not just what happened but how you felt about it, what it reminds you of, and what it means to you.

This type of writing often involves multiple sessions on the same topic. You might write about a relationship conflict, a work situation, or a loss several times, each session revealing new layers of understanding. The goal isn't to "*solve*" the situation but to fully experience and integrate your emotional response to it.

3. **Gratitude and Appreciation Journaling:**

While processing difficult emotions is important, balance comes from also acknowledging what's working in your life. Gratitude journaling, such as writing about things you appreciate, moments of beauty you've noticed, or people who have touched your life, can help rewire your brain toward noticing positive experiences.

The key to effective gratitude journaling is specificity. Rather than writing

"I'm grateful for my family," you might write *"I'm grateful for the way my daughter laughed at her own joke this morning, and how that sound made me feel connected to pure joy."* This specificity helps your brain really absorb and encode the positive experience.

4. **Dialogue Journaling:**

Sometimes it's helpful to have conversations on paper with different aspects of yourself or with people in your life (whether or not you ever share these conversations with them). You might write a dialogue between your anxious self and your wise self, or between your current self and your future self. You might write letters to people you need to forgive, to forgive you, or to thank.

This type of journaling can help you access different perspectives on your situation and practice conversations you might want to have in real life. It can also help you connect with your own inner wisdom and compassion.

5. **Reflection and Insight Journaling:**

This involves looking back on your experiences and extracting meaning, lessons, or patterns. You might write about what you learned from a difficult period, how you've grown over the past year, or what patterns you notice in your relationships or reactions.

This type of journaling often happens best with some distance from events, such as writing about something that happened last week, last month, or last year rather than something that's happening right now. The goal is integration and wisdom rather than immediate emotional release.

The Practice: Meeting Yourself on Paper

Let's walk through how to establish a journaling practice that serves your emotional well-being and mental clarity. Like any healing practice, the key is consistency rather than perfection, and self-compassion rather than self-criticism.

Beginning Your Session:

Start each journaling session with a moment of transition. Take a few deep breaths, notice how you're feeling in your body, and set an intention for your writing time. This might be as simple as "*I want to understand what I'm feeling right now*" or "*I want to clear my mind of today's worries.*"

Some people find it helpful to begin each session with the same prompt: "*Right now I'm feeling...*" or "*What's on my mind today is...*" This creates a bridge between your internal experience and the page, helping you transition from everyday consciousness to the more reflective state that supports healing writing.

The Writing Itself:

Once you begin writing, try to maintain continuous movement across the page. This doesn't mean writing frantically, but rather not stopping to edit, correct, or judge what's emerging. If you're not sure what to write next, describe what you're experiencing in that moment: "*I'm sitting here not knowing what to write, feeling a little anxious about...*"

Don't worry about grammar, spelling, or whether what you're writing is "*good*" or "*important.*" The value of therapeutic journaling lies in the process of expression and exploration, not in the quality of the final product. Some of your most healing writing might be messy, repetitive, or seemingly incoherent.

Dealing with Difficult Emotions:

When intense emotions arise during writing, it's important to stay present with them while also maintaining your emotional safety. If you notice yourself becoming overwhelmed, you can:

- Slow down your writing pace

- Take breaks to breathe deeply
- Write about the emotion itself: *"I'm feeling scared right now, and that fear feels like..."*
- Remind yourself that you're safe in this moment
- End the session if needed and return to it later

Remember that the goal isn't to solve everything in one session, but rather to create space for your emotional experience to be witnessed and expressed.

Closing Your Session:

End each writing session consciously rather than just stopping when you run out of time. You might write a brief summary of what you discovered, express gratitude for insights that emerged, or set an intention for carrying forward what you learned.

Some people find it helpful to read back through what they wrote, while others prefer to close the journal without reviewing. Trust your instincts about what feels most supportive for your process.

Building Your Personal Writing Practice

Establishing a sustainable journaling practice is like tending a garden, it requires patience, consistency, and trust in the process. The goal is to create a practice that feels supportive rather than burdensome, healing rather than stressful.

1. **Start Small:** Begin with just 10-15 minutes of writing, three times per week. This might seem modest, but consistency is more important than duration, especially in the beginning. Many people find that once they start, they naturally want to write longer or more frequently because of

how good it makes them feel.

2. **Choose Your Tools:** Some people prefer the tactile experience of pen and paper, finding that the physical act of handwriting slows down their thoughts and creates a more meditative experience. Others prefer typing, especially if they write faster than they can think and want to capture streams of consciousness.

3. Experiment with different options: a beautiful journal that feels special, a simple notebook that feels approachable, or a password-protected document on your computer. What matters is that your tools feel good to you and support rather than hinder your expression.

4. **Create Ritual:** Consider developing small rituals around your journaling practice that help signal to your brain that this is important, restorative time. This might be lighting a candle, making a cup of tea, or taking three deep breaths before you begin. These rituals help create a sense of sacred time and space for your inner work.

5. **Be Patient with the Process:** Some journaling sessions will feel profound and insightful, while others might feel mundane or repetitive. Both types of sessions are valuable. The healing doesn't only happen during the dramatic breakthroughs—it also happens through the quiet, consistent witnessing of your inner experience.

Trust that the practice is working even when you can't see immediate results. Like physical exercise, the benefits of journaling are often cumulative, becoming apparent over weeks and months rather than individual sessions.

The Digital Age and Written Reflection

In our screen-saturated world, the choice between digital and analog journaling deserves special consideration. Both approaches have unique benefits and potential drawbacks for therapeutic writing.

Handwritten Journaling engages different neural pathways than typing, often leading to slower, more thoughtful expression. The physical act of forming letters can be meditative, and research suggests that handwriting may enhance memory and emotional processing. There's also something satisfying about the permanence of ink on paper and the inability to endlessly edit your thoughts. However, handwritten journaling can be slower, potentially limiting your ability to keep up with rapid thoughts or emotions. Some people also worry about privacy if their journal could be found and read by others.

Digital Journaling allows for faster expression, which can be helpful when you're processing intense emotions or have limited time. Digital journals can be password-protected, easily searchable, and accessible from multiple devices. They also eliminate concerns about handwriting legibility or running out of pages. The downside is that digital devices come with built-in distractions, such as notifications, other apps, and the temptation to multitask. The screen light can also be stimulating rather than calming, especially for evening writing sessions.

Consider experimenting with both approaches to see what serves your particular nervous system and lifestyle. Some people use hybrid approaches: handwriting for morning reflection and digital for quick evening processing, or alternating based on their current needs and circumstances.

Every time you choose to process your emotions on paper rather than carrying them as tension in your body, you're practicing excellent self-care. Every time you use writing to understand yourself more deeply, you're investing in your emotional intelligence and resilience. Every time you create space for your inner voice to be heard, you're honoring the full complexity of your human experience. The page is waiting to meet you exactly where you are. Your story is worth telling, especially to yourself. Your next conversation with your own deepest wisdom is just a pen stroke away.

Tracking Your Journaling Journey

What to Notice:

- Emotional shifts before, during, and after writing
- Patterns in your thoughts and feelings over time
- Insights or revelations that emerge through writing
- Changes in your ability to process difficult emotions
- How journaling affects your relationships and daily interactions
- Which types of writing feel most beneficial for different situations

Journaling Practice Log:

Date: _________ **Time:** _________ **Duration:** _________

Setting: ☐ Morning pages ☐ Evening reflection ☐ Crisis processing ☐ Gratitude focus ☐ Stream of consciousness ☐ Emotional exploration ☐

Other: ____

Before writing:

Emotional state: ______________________________________

Stress level (1-10): ___________________________________

Mental clarity (1-10): _____________

What's on my mind: _______________

After writing:

Emotional state: _______________

Stress level (1-10): _____________

Mental clarity (1-10): ___________

How I feel about the session: _______________

What I wrote about: ☐ Current stress or worry ☐ Relationship issue ☐ Past experience/memory ☐ Future hopes or fears ☐ Daily experiences ☐ Gratitude and appreciation ☐ Decision I'm trying to make ☐ Emotions I needed to process ☐ Stream of consciousness ☐ Other:

____

Insights or breakthroughs:

Emotions that arose during writing: ☐ Relief ☐ Sadness ☐ Anger ☐ Joy ☐ Confusion ☐ Clarity ☐ Anxiety ☐ Peace ☐ Frustration ☐ Gratitude ☐ Other: ________________

How I handled difficult emotions: ☐ Stayed present with them ☐ Took breaks ☐ Wrote about the emotions themselves ☐ Needed to stop early ☐ Felt supported by the process ☐ Other: ______________________

Most meaningful part of this session:

____

____

____

____

____

How this writing might influence my day/week:

____

____

What I want to explore in future sessions:

Weekly Reflection: What themes keep appearing in your writing? How has your emotional relationship with difficult topics changed through journaling? What types of writing serve you best during different moods or circumstances? How is regular self-expression affecting your overall well-being and relationships?

5

Sip Herbal Tea

The Gentle Medicine in Your Cup

In our hurried world of instant everything; instant coffee, instant messages, instant gratification, we've somehow forgotten the profound pleasure of slowing down for a simple cup of tea. Not the grab-and-go variety that we gulp while checking emails, but the kind of tea drinking that our grandmothers knew: a deliberate pause, a moment of warmth, a gentle ritual that says "*I'm taking care of myself right now.*"

There's something almost magical about the transformation that happens when you pour hot water over dried herbs and watch the liquid change color, releasing fragrant steam that carries with it the promise of calm. It's alchemy happening right in your kitchen; simple plants becoming liquid comfort, stress dissolving into steam.

If you've ever found yourself automatically reaching for another cup of coffee when you're feeling frazzled, only to end up more jittery and anxious, you've experienced firsthand how what we drink affects how we feel. Today, we're going to explore how switching that automatic response from stimulation to soothing can become one of your most reliable tools for finding calm in the chaos of daily life.

This isn't about becoming a tea snob or investing in expensive equipment. It's about discovering how a simple, warm beverage can become a bridge between the stressed-out version of yourself and the calmer, more centered person you're capable of being. It's about learning to use tea not just as a drink, but as a form of liquid meditation, a pause button for your nervous system, and a gentle way to show yourself care.

The Ancient Wisdom in Modern Times

Long before we had pharmaceutical solutions for anxiety and stress, humans turned to plants for healing. Tea drinking isn't just a pleasant habit, it's one of humanity's oldest forms of medicine. For thousands of years, people have known that certain plants, when steeped in hot water, can calm the mind, soothe the stomach, and help the body find its natural state of ease.

Traditional Chinese medicine has used herbal teas for over 4,000 years, understanding that what we consume affects not just our physical health but our emotional well-being. European folk medicine relied heavily on herbal teas to treat everything from insomnia to digestive upset to nervous tension. Indigenous cultures around the world developed sophisticated tea traditions, knowing which plants brought peace, which sparked energy, and which helped during times of grief or stress.

What's remarkable is that modern science is now proving what traditional healers always knew: these plants really do have the power to change how we feel. The compounds in herbal teas; flavonoids, essential oils, amino acids, interact with our neurotransmitters and nervous system in measurable ways. We're not just drinking flavored water; we're consuming gentle medicine that's been tested by thousands of years of human experience.

Perhaps even more importantly, the ritual of tea drinking itself has therapeutic value. In our multitasking culture, tea drinking forces us to slow down, to wait, to be present with the process of brewing and sipping. It creates what researchers call a "*mindful pause,*" a brief respite from the constant doing that characterizes modern life.

Why Herbal Tea Works: The Power of Plants

Herbal teas like chamomile and peppermint are more than just delicious—they are packed with natural properties that help reduce anxiety, improve digestion, and promote better sleep. Studies have shown that chamomile can help lower stress levels by acting as a mild sedative (Zick et al., 2011), while peppermint has been linked to improved relaxation and reduced muscle tension (McKay & Blumberg, 2006).

When you sip on a cup of tea, you're not only benefiting from the active compounds in the herbs, but the process itself can become a mini-meditation. The act of preparing and enjoying tea allows you to slow down, take a breath, and center yourself; an important aspect of any stress-management strategy.

The Science of Soothing Sips

When you sip a cup of chamomile tea and feel your shoulders relax, you're not imagining things. There's actual biochemistry happening in your body that's shifting you from stress to calm. Understanding this process can help you appreciate why something as simple as herbal tea can be such a powerful tool for emotional regulation.

The active compounds in calming herbs work on your nervous system in several ways. Chamomile, for instance, contains apigenin, a flavonoid that binds to benzodiazepine receptors in your brain; the same receptors that anti-anxiety medications target, though much more gently. This binding helps reduce neural activity and promotes feelings of calm and drowsiness.

L-theanine, found in green tea and some herbal blends, increases the production of GABA, serotonin, and dopamine, are neurotransmitters that promote relaxation and mood stability. Studies show that L-theanine can reduce cortisol levels and help shift brain waves toward the alpha state associated with calm alertness.

Your Personal Tea Pharmacy

Not all herbal teas are created equal when it comes to stress relief, and different herbs serve different purposes in your emotional toolkit. Think of your tea collection as a gentle pharmacy, each herb offering its own particular form of support for different moods and moments.

Chamomile is perhaps the most well-known calming tea, and for good reason. This gentle herb has been used for centuries to soothe anxiety, promote sleep, and calm digestive upset that often accompanies stress. Chamomile is particularly helpful if your stress manifests as racing thoughts or difficulty winding down at the end of the day. It's mild enough to drink regularly and safe for most people, making it an excellent foundation for your calming tea practice.

Lavender brings the spa experience right to your cup. Its floral scent alone can trigger relaxation responses, and when consumed as tea, it can help reduce anxiety and promote deeper sleep. Lavender tea is particularly beneficial if you're dealing with tension headaches or need help transitioning from day to evening. The aroma therapy aspect makes it especially powerful, you're getting benefits from both drinking and inhaling.

Peppermint offers a different kind of calm, the clarity that comes from cooling inflammation and soothing digestive distress. If your stress tends to hit you in the stomach or if you feel mentally foggy when overwhelmed, peppermint can provide refreshing relief. It's also excellent for headaches and can help you feel more alert while still relaxed.

Lemon Balm is a member of the mint family that's particularly effective for nervous tension and restlessness. It has a gentle, citrusy flavor and can help if you're feeling overstimulated or having trouble focusing. Lemon balm is especially good for stress that manifests as irritability or social anxiety.

Passionflower has been used traditionally for anxiety and insomnia, and modern research supports its calming effects. It's particularly helpful if your mind tends to race or if you have trouble letting go of worries. The tea has a mild, grassy flavor and can be especially beneficial in the evening.

Holy Basil (Tulsi) is considered an adaptogen, an herb that helps your body manage stress more effectively over time. It has a complex, slightly spicy flavor and can help regulate cortisol levels. Tulsi is particularly beneficial if you're dealing with chronic stress or need support for overall resilience.

Ginger and Turmeric teas offer anti-inflammatory benefits that can help address the physical effects of chronic stress. If stress is showing up as body aches, digestive issues, or general inflammation, these warming spices can provide both comfort and healing.

Many commercial tea blends combine several of these herbs to create synergistic effects. "*Sleepytime*" blends often combine chamomile, passionflower, and lemon balm. "*Stress relief*" teas might include lavender, chamomile, and holy basil. Don't be afraid to experiment with different combinations to find what works best for your particular stress patterns.

Step-by-Step: How to Sip Herbal Tea for Maximum Calm

Here's how to incorporate herbal tea into your stress-relief routine:

1. Choose Your Tea: Pick a calming herbal tea. Chamomile, peppermint, lemon balm, and lavender are all excellent choices for relaxation. You may even want to try a blend designed specifically for stress relief.

2. Brew the Tea: Boil water and steep your tea bag or loose leaves according to the instructions on the package. Let the tea steep long enough for the flavors and active compounds to infuse the water, typically 5-7 minutes.

3. Find a Quiet Spot: Once your tea is ready, find a comfortable place to sit and relax. This could be your favorite chair, a spot by the window, or a cozy nook where you can unwind without distractions.

4. Savor Each Sip: As you sip the tea, take a moment to really experience it. Feel the warmth as it soothes your hands and sip slowly, noticing the flavors and aroma. Allow yourself to be present in the moment, letting go of any stress or tension.

5. Breathe Deeply: As you enjoy your tea, take slow, deep breaths. Inhale deeply through your nose, hold for a moment, and exhale fully. This deep breathing enhances the calming effects of the tea and helps you relax even further.

Tracking Your Tea Practice

What to Notice:

- Which herbs feel most calming for your particular stress patterns
- How your mood shifts before, during, and after tea time
- Changes in your sleep quality with evening herbal tea
- Whether the ritual itself (preparation, sipping) affects your stress levels
- How regular tea practice influences your overall relationship with self-care
- Physical sensations of relaxation as you drink

Tea Practice Log:

Date: _________ **Time:** _________ **Duration:** _________

Current stress level (1-10): _____ **Energy level (1-10):** _____

Type of tea: ☐ Chamomile ☐ Lavender ☐ Peppermint ☐ Lemon Balm ☐ Passionflower ☐ Holy Basil ☐ Ginger ☐ Custom blend ☐ Other: _______________

Setting: ☐ Morning ritual ☐ Workday break ☐ Afternoon pause ☐ Evening wind-down ☐ Crisis moment ☐ Other: _______________

How I prepared: ☐ Rushed through it ☐ Mindful preparation ☐ Enjoyed the process ☐ Used special cup/space ☐ Other: _______________

During tea time I: ☐ Sat quietly and focused on drinking ☐ Multitasked ☐ Watched steam/color change ☐ Practiced gratitude ☐ Let my mind wander peacefully ☐ Focused on breathing ☐ Other: _______________

After tea: Stress level (1-10): _____ **Energy level (1-10):** _____
Mood: ____

Physical sensations I noticed: ☐ Shoulders relaxed ☐ Breathing deepened ☐ Tension released ☐ Warmth spreading ☐ Digestive calm ☐ Headache relief ☐ Other: ______________________________

Mental/emotional shifts: ☐ Thoughts slowed down ☐ Felt more centered ☐ Increased clarity ☐ Mood lifted ☐ Anxiety decreased ☐ Felt cared for ☐ Other: ___________________________________

What I appreciated about this tea time: ____________________

____

____

____

How this practice might influence the rest of my day:

____

____

____

____

Notes about taste/preparation preferences:

____

____

____

____

Weekly Reflection: Which teas are becoming your favorites? How is regular tea practice affecting your overall stress levels? What patterns do you notice about when you most crave this ritual? How is this simple practice changing your relationship with self-care?

6

Warm Bath or Shower

There's something deeply primal about the comfort of warm water. Think about it, we spent our very first months floating in the warm, protective waters of the womb, completely safe and utterly relaxed. Perhaps that's why even the most stressed-out adult can sink into a warm bath and feel some ancient part of themselves remember what it means to truly let go.

If you've ever noticed how your shoulders automatically drop when you step into a hot shower after a brutal day, or how your mind finally quiets when you slip into a warm bath, you've experienced something that cultures around the world have known for millennia: water has the power to wash away more than just physical dirt, it can cleanse away tension, stress, and the accumulated weight of the day. But here's what many people don't realize: there's a science to turning your bath or shower from a routine hygiene task into a powerful stress-relief ritual. When you understand how warm water affects your nervous system, you can transform these daily moments into profound opportunities for healing and restoration.

Why Warm Water Works: The Science of Liquid Therapy

Let's dig into the fascinating biology of what happens when your body meets warm water. It's not just about feeling good, though that certainly matters, it's about triggering many physiological responses that actively counteract stress. When you immerse yourself in warm water, several remarkable things happen simultaneously. First, the heat causes your blood vessels to dilate, improving circulation throughout your body. This enhanced blood flow delivers fresh oxygen and nutrients to tense muscles while carrying away metabolic waste products that contribute to stiffness and soreness. It's like giving your circulatory system a gentle, full-body massage.

The warmth also triggers your body's relaxation response through what scientists call thermotherapy. Research published in the Journal of Applied Physiology shows that warm water immersion activates your parasympathetic nervous system, the same "*rest and digest*" system that box breathing targets. Your heart rate naturally slows, your blood pressure drops, and your body begins producing fewer stress hormones like cortisol and adrenaline. But the magic goes deeper. Warm water stimulates the release of endorphins; your body's natural "*feel-good*" chemicals. These are the same substances released during exercise or laughter, but you're getting them simply by soaking in warm water.

A study from the University of Freiburg found that people who took regular warm baths showed significant improvements in mood and reductions in symptoms of depression and anxiety. The heat also affects your muscles in many significant ways. When muscle fibers warm up, they become more pliable and less prone to spasm. This is why physical therapists often use heat therapy for treating muscle tension and pain. The warm water essentially helps your muscles "*remember*" how to relax, breaking the cycle of tension that stress creates.

There's also something called the "diving response" that occurs when you're immersed in water. Your body instinctively slows down your heart rate and redirects blood flow to essential organs, creating a natural state of calm alertness. It's an evolutionary response that helps mammals conserve energy in water, but for humans, it translates into a deeply relaxing experience.

Japanese researchers studying the effects of bathing culture found that people who took regular warm baths had lower levels of inflammatory markers in their blood and better sleep quality compared to those who only showered. The practice of "*forest bathing*" in Japan isn't just about being in nature, it's about the meditative, restorative quality of immersion that warm water provides.

The Ritual That Travels From Ancient Times to Your Bathroom

Humans have been using warm water for healing and relaxation for thousands of years. The ancient Romans built elaborate bathhouses not just for cleanliness, but as centers of social and therapeutic life. The Japanese have elevated bathing to an art form with their onsen (hot spring) culture, where the act of bathing is considered essential for both physical and spiritual well-being.

In Finland, the sauna tradition combines heat and water in a ritual that's been shown to reduce stress hormones and improve cardiovascular health. Native American sweat lodge ceremonies use steam and water for purification and emotional release. Across cultures and throughout history, warm water has been recognized as a powerful tool for healing.

What makes warm baths and showers so universally appealing is their accessibility. Unlike many stress-relief techniques that require special training or equipment, most of us have access to warm water. You don't need a fancy spa or expensive treatments, your own bathroom can become a sanctuary of calm with just a few intentional adjustments.

The beauty of this practice lies in its dual nature: it's both incredibly simple and surprisingly profound. You can have a quick, stress-relieving shower in five minutes, or you can create an elaborate bath ritual that lasts an hour. Both approaches offer genuine benefits, and you can adapt the practice to fit your schedule, space, and preferences.

Why Warm Water Works: The Science Behind the Soothing Effects

When you immerse yourself in warm water, it has a direct impact on your body's physiology. Studies have shown that warm water helps to relax muscles, increase blood flow, and reduce tension in the body, which all contribute to reducing stress. The heat promotes vasodilation (the widening of blood vessels), which improves circulation and helps to flush out metabolic waste products, leaving you feeling refreshed and relaxed (Matsumoto et al., 2007).

Beyond the physical benefits, warm water has a profound impact on your mental state. Research suggests that a warm bath can stimulate the production of oxytocin, the hormone associated with bonding and relaxation, helping to alleviate anxiety and promote feelings of calm (Nagata et al., 2012). In short, a warm bath or shower is a simple yet effective way to engage both your body and mind in the relaxation process.

Step-by-Step: How to Maximize the Relaxing Benefits of a Warm Bath or Shower

Let's take a look at how you can use a warm bath or shower to relieve stress and relax your body:

1. Prepare Your Space: Whether you're running a bath or setting up for a shower, create an environment that promotes relaxation. Dim the lights, add a few calming essential oils or bath salts, and turn on some soft, soothing music if that helps you unwind.

2. Set the Temperature: The water should be warm enough to relax your muscles but not too hot to cause discomfort. For most people, a temperature of around 100-104°F (37-40°C) is ideal.

3. Soak or Shower: If you're taking a bath, sink into the water and let it envelop you. If you're in the shower, take time to feel the water flow over your body and focus on the sensation. Close your eyes and take deep, calming breaths as you let go of the stress of the day.

4. Focus on Relaxation: As you soak or shower, let go of any tension in your body. Pay attention to how your muscles begin to relax as the warmth eases away tightness. Imagine the water washing away any stress or negativity you're holding onto.

5. Breathe Deeply: Use this time to engage in deep breathing. Inhale slowly through your nose, hold for a moment, and exhale through your mouth. This simple practice can help calm your nervous system and enhance the relaxation effects of the warm water.

As you begin to explore warm water as a stress-relief tool, remember that you're tapping into one of humanity's oldest and most universal healing practices. Every culture that has had access to warm water has discovered its power to soothe, heal, and restore. Be patient with yourself as you learn what works best for you. Some days, a quick warm shower will be exactly what you need. Other days, you might crave a long, luxurious bath with all the enhancements. Both approaches are valid and valuable.

Don't worry about doing it "*perfectly.*" The most important thing is that you're taking time to care for yourself. Whether your bath is interrupted by a phone call, or your shower is shorter than planned, or you forget to add the Epsom salts, these imperfections don't diminish the value of what you're doing.

Pay attention to how you feel before and after your warm water sessions. Notice patterns in when you most need this type of care, and how different approaches affect your mood and stress levels. This awareness will help you use warm water therapy most effectively.

Your relationship with stress and self-care is unique, and your warm water practice should reflect that uniqueness. Trust your instincts about what feels good and what doesn't. Your body has wisdom about what it needs, warm water therapy is simply a tool for accessing and honoring that wisdom.

Take a moment right now to imagine stepping into a warm, soothing bath or shower. Picture the water flowing over your shoulders, feel your muscles beginning to relax, notice your breathing naturally slowing down. That feeling of relief and comfort is always available to you, it's just a faucet turn away. Your warm water sanctuary awaits. Use it generously, use it mindfully, and most importantly, use it as an act of kindness toward yourself.

Tracking Your Warm Water Practice

What to Notice:

- Your stress level before and after (1-10 scale)
- Physical sensations during and after (muscle tension, circulation, overall comfort)
- Emotional state changes (mood, anxiety level, sense of peace)
- Water temperature and duration that worked best
- Any additions that enhanced the experience (salts, oils, music)
- Sleep quality on nights you used warm water therapy
- Times of day when the practice felt most beneficial

Warm Water Therapy Practice Log:

Date: _________ **Time:** _________ **Type:** Bath / Shower

Duration: _________

Stress Level Before: 1-10_______________________________________

Stress Level After: 1-10____

Water Temperature: ☐ Too Cool ☐ Just Right ☐ Too Hot

Duration: ☐ Too Short ☐ Just Right ☐ Too Long

Enhancements Used: ☐ Epsom salts ☐ Essential oils ☐ Candles ☐ Music ☐ Silence ☐ Other: ___________

What I noticed: ☐ Muscles felt less tense ☐ Mind felt quieter ☐ Breathed more deeply ☐ Felt emotionally lighter ☐ Became sleepy/relaxed ☐ Wanted to stay longer ☐ Felt more connected to my body ☐ Gained new perspective on problems

Best part of this session: _________________________________

What I'd change next time: _________________________________

How did I sleep that night? ☐ Better ☐ Same ☐ Worse ☐ Not applicable

Will I use this approach again? ☐ Definitely ☐ Maybe ☐ Probably not

Weekly Reflection:

After practicing for a week, what patterns do you notice? When is warm water therapy most helpful for you? What temperature, duration, and enhancements work best? How has regular practice affected your overall stress levels and sleep quality?

7

Progressive Muscle Relaxation

Your Body's Stress-Free Reset Button

We carry stress in our bodies without even realizing it. Whether it's the tightness in your shoulders after a long day at the desk or the tension in your jaw after an argument, physical stress has a way of silently accumulating. Progressive Muscle Relaxation (PMR) is a simple yet effective technique to release this built-up tension. By systematically tensing and relaxing different muscle groups, you're teaching your body how to unwind, one muscle at a time. The beauty of PMR lies in its simplicity. It's a straightforward way to help you reconnect with your body, release physical stress, and regain a sense of calm. It's like giving your muscles permission to finally take a break.

Why Progressive Muscle Relaxation Works: The Science of Letting Go

When we're stressed, our bodies instinctively tighten up, almost like a protective mechanism. But when you deliberately tense and then relax your muscles, you're not only releasing physical stress, but you're also telling your brain that it's safe to let go. By practicing PMR, you're essentially resetting your body's stress response.

Studies show that PMR can lower heart rate, reduce blood pressure, and even enhance sleep quality. One study found that people who practiced PMR regularly reported lower levels of anxiety and higher levels of mental clarity, making it a powerful tool for both physical and emotional well-being.

Step-by-Step: Your Progressive Muscle Relaxation Routine

Let's walk through the process of Progressive Muscle Relaxation, so you can start releasing stress right now:

1. **Get Comfortable**: Find a quiet, comfortable spot to sit or lie down. Close your eyes and take a few deep breaths to settle into the moment.

2. **Focus on Your Feet**: Start with your feet. Tense the muscles in your feet as tightly as you can, hold for a few seconds, and then slowly release. Pay attention to how the muscles feel as they relax.

3. **Move Upward**: Gradually work your way up the body, focusing on each muscle group—your calves, thighs, stomach, chest, arms, neck, and face. For each muscle group, tense, hold, and release. Focus on the sensation of relief as the tension fades.

4. **Mindful Breathing**: As you tense and release, remember to breathe slowly and deeply. Inhale as you tense and exhale as you release.

5. **Finish with Awareness**: After you've worked through your entire body, take a few moments to lie still and notice how your body feels. Do you feel lighter, more relaxed? Take a mental note of your physical and emotional state.

Tracking Your Progressive Muscle Relaxation Practice
What to Notice:

- Your stress level before and after (1-10 scale)
- Which muscle groups felt the most tense

- Any physical sensations or relief you noticed
- Whether your mind wandered during the practice
- The best times of day for your relaxation practice
- Situations where PMR was most/least helpful

Progressive Muscle Relaxation Practice Log:

Date: _________ **Time:** _________ **Location:** _________________

Duration: _________

Stress Level Before: 1-10_____________

Stress Level After: 1-10_______________

Muscle groups that felt most tense: ______________

What I noticed: ☐ Mind wandered ☐ Felt physically calmer ☐ Tension released ☐ Hard to focus on relaxation ☐ Felt sleepy/relaxed ☐ Wanted to continue longer

Best part of this session: __________________________________

What I'd change next time: ________________________________
Will I use this technique again? ☐ Definitely ☐ Maybe ☐ Probably not

Weekly Reflection:

After practicing for a week, what patterns do you notice? When is PMR most helpful for you? What adjustments have you made to make it work better?

8

The Role of Music & Exercise

Your Energy-Boosting Power Combo

There's something about the rhythm of music that makes you want to move, right? Maybe it's the beat that gets your feet tapping or the lyrics that spark a little joy. Combine that with the rush of exercise, and you've got a powerful combo for boosting your mood and energy. This chapter is all about harnessing the magic of music and movement to elevate your emotional well-being, turning your workout into an uplifting experience that leaves you feeling better than before.

Think about it: when you hear your favorite upbeat song, it's hard to resist the urge to move. Whether it's a dance, a jog, or simply grooving to the beat, moving your body to music can instantly shift your mood and energize you. By the end of this chapter, you'll know how to use music and exercise together to create a more joyful, energetic you.

Why Music and Exercise Work: The Perfect Pairing

Exercise is known for its ability to release endorphins, those feel-good chemicals in your brain that instantly improve your mood. When combined with music, which also has the power to boost emotional well-being, you create a synergy that's hard to beat. Studies show that music can amplify the positive effects of exercise by making you feel more motivated and enhancing the release of those mood-lifting chemicals. The upbeat rhythms can help you push harder, while the music makes the whole experience more enjoyable. The beauty of this combo is that it doesn't matter whether you're running, dancing, or doing a yoga flow, just adding your favorite tunes can take your workout from "*meh*" to "*wow*."

Step-by-Step: How to Move to the Beat

Let's dig in and use the power of music to fuel your exercise routine:

1. **Choose Your Playlist**: Pick music that makes you want to move. Whether it's high-energy pop, dance beats, or motivational tracks, the key is to find something that lifts your spirits and gets you moving.

2. **Get Moving**: Start with a warm-up, then let the music guide you. Dance, jog in place, do jumping jacks, or whatever movement feels good to you. The goal is to let loose and move with the rhythm of the music. Don't worry about looking perfect, just have fun!

3. **Increase the Intensity**: As the beat picks up, increase your pace or intensity. Push yourself a little harder as the music energizes you. Let the music be your motivation.

4. **Cool Down**: After you've danced or moved energetically, slow down with some gentle stretches to help your body recover.

Tracking Your Music-Exercise Practice

What to Notice:

- Your stress level before and after (1-10 scale)
- How the music impacted your energy levels

- The movements you enjoyed most
- Any physical sensations or relief you noticed
- Whether the music motivated you to push harder or move longer
- The best times of day for this activity

Music-Exercise Practice Log:

Date: _________ **Time:** _________ **Location:** _________________

Duration: _________

Stress Level Before: 1-10_____________________________________

Stress Level After: 1-10______________________________________

Music that energized me: ____________________________________

What I noticed: ☐ Felt more energized ☐ Enjoyed the movement ☐ Music motivated me ☐ Hard to keep up with the beat ☐ Felt more positive ☐ Wanted to keep going longer

Best part of this session: ___________________________________

What I'd change next time: _________________________________

Will I use this technique again? ☐ Definitely ☐ Maybe ☐ Probably not

Weekly Reflection:

After practicing for a week, what patterns do you notice? When is music-exercise most helpful for you? What adjustments have you made to make it work better?

9

Gratitude List

Your Simple Path to Positivity

It's easy to get caught up in the high-demand of everyday life, letting stress, frustrations, and challenges take center stage. But what if we told you that one of the most effective ways to shift your mindset and improve your emotional well-being could be as simple as writing down a few things you're thankful for each day? Gratitude lists may sound basic, but they hold the power to transform your outlook and reduce stress, making you more resilient in the face of life's ups and downs.

Cultivating gratitude isn't just a feel-good habit, it's a powerful tool for shifting your focus from what's wrong to what's right in your life. By regularly practicing gratitude, you're creating a mental habit that trains you to notice the good, even when things aren't going perfectly. It's a simple, but deeply effective, way to make positivity a natural part of your daily routine.

Why Gratitude Works: The Science Behind the Shift

The practice of gratitude has been linked to improved mental health and well-being. Research shows that when we take time to focus on the things we're grateful for, we train our brains to recognize the positive aspects of life more easily. This shift in focus not only helps reduce feelings of stress and anxiety, but it also promotes a greater sense of resilience and happiness.

Gratitude is a powerful antidote to negative emotions. Studies have shown that people who regularly practice gratitude experience lower levels of depression and higher levels of overall life satisfaction. By simply making a habit of acknowledging the good in our lives, we create a buffer against stress and a greater sense of joy.

Step-by-Step: Your Gratitude Practice

Let's make gratitude a part of your routine with this simple practice:

1. **Set Aside Time**: Take a moment each day, whether in the morning, before bed, or whenever feels right for you. Find a quiet place where you can reflect without distractions.

2. **Write Your List**: Write down 3-5 things you're grateful for. They don't have to be big things. Sometimes, it's the small moments that make the most impact. It could be a good cup of coffee, a kind word from a friend, or the quiet moments of peace you find in your day.

3. **Reflect**: As you write, take a moment to really feel the gratitude. Reflect on why these things bring you joy, and let the feeling of appreciation fill you up.

4. **Revisit Your List**: Whenever you're feeling stressed, revisit your list and let the positive energy flow back in. You can even add to it as you notice new things you're thankful for.

Tracking Your Gratitude Practice

What to Notice:

- Your stress level before and after (1-10 scale)
- Any shifts in your mood or outlook
- Whether writing down things you're grateful for made you feel more positive or calmer
- The types of things you're grateful for (big or small)
- How often you notice new things to add to your list
- The best times of day for your gratitude practice

Gratitude Practice Log:

Date: _________ **Time:** _________ **Location:** ____________________

Duration: _________
Stress Level Before: 1-10____________________________

Stress Level After: 1-10_____________________________
Things I'm Grateful For:

____

____

____

____

____

____

What I noticed: ☐ Felt more positive ☐ Felt calmer ☐ Shifted my focus from stress ☐ Realized how much I have to be thankful for

Best part of this session: ______________________________________

____

What I'd change next time: ________________________________

Will I use this technique again? ☐ Definitely ☐ Maybe ☐ Probably not

Weekly Reflection:

After practicing for a week, what patterns do you notice? When is gratitude most helpful for you? What adjustments have you made to make it work better?

10

Do a Brain Dump

Your Mental Clean-Up Strategy

Have you ever felt like your mind is racing, with a million thoughts all demanding your attention at once? Maybe you're thinking about work, personal obligations, things to do, or even random worries that pop into your head out of nowhere. It can feel like mental clutter piling up, leaving you overwhelmed and unable to focus. That's where a brain dump comes in. This simple practice is a way to clear out the mental fog and regain control of your thoughts.

A brain dump involves writing down everything that's been taking up space in your mind. By putting your thoughts on paper, you free up your brain to focus on the things that truly matter. It's like giving your mind a break and allowing it to breathe again, making it easier to process emotions and clear away mental clutter.

Why a Brain Dump Works: The Power of Letting Go

When your mind is overloaded with thoughts, it can be hard to think clearly or make decisions. The brain dump is a simple, effective tool for decluttering your mental space. By writing everything down, you give yourself permission to release those thoughts and worries, preventing them from running on a loop in your head.

The beauty of brain dumping is that it's not about organizing or making sense of everything right away. It's about clearing the mental space so you can approach problems with a fresh perspective. Research suggests that this kind of mental release helps reduce anxiety, improve focus, and bring clarity to your thoughts.

Step-by-Step: How to Do a Brain Dump

Let's go through the steps so you can experience the power of a brain dump yourself:

1. **Find a Quiet Space**: Choose a place where you won't be interrupted. Sit down with a pen and paper or open a blank document on your device.

2. **Set a Timer**: Give yourself 5-10 minutes to write. The time limit helps you focus and prevents you from getting stuck in your thoughts.

3. **Write Everything Down**: Write down whatever is on your mind. There are no rules; don't worry about punctuation, grammar, or structure. Let the thoughts flow freely, from the big stuff to the small stuff.

4. **Don't Hold Back**: Even if it seems trivial or silly, write it down. The goal is to release everything that's occupying your mind.

5. **Review (Optional)**: After the timer goes off, take a moment to look over what you've written. You don't have to organize or make sense of it right away, but notice if any themes or important points stand out.

Tracking Your Brain Dump Practice

What to Notice:

- Your stress level before and after (1-10 scale)

- Whether you feel lighter or more relaxed after the dump
- What thoughts or worries seem to come up most frequently
- Whether any solutions or insights come to mind after the dump
- How your ability to focus improves after doing a brain dump
- The best times of day for this practice

Brain Dump Practice Log:

Date: _________ **Time:** _________ **Location:** _________________

Duration: _______________

Stress Level Before: 1-10_______________________

Stress Level After: 1-10________________________

What I wrote about: ________________________________

What I noticed: ☐ Felt lighter ☐ Thoughts became clearer ☐ Realized I had too much on my plate ☐ Felt more focused ☐ Felt a sense of relief

Best part of this session: ___________________________________

What I'd change next time: ________________________________

Will I use this technique again? ☐ Definitely ☐ Maybe ☐ Probably not

Weekly Reflection:
After practicing for a week, what patterns do you notice? What topics or concerns appear the most in your brain dumps? How has brain dumping impacted your ability to focus and stay calm?

11

Stretch

Your Simple Path to Tension Release

We all carry stress in our bodies, whether it's in tight shoulders after a long day at the desk or in a stiff neck after a stressful meeting. Stretching is one of the easiest and most effective ways to release that tension. It's not just about flexibility; it's about giving your muscles the space to relax and breathe again. This chapter is all about helping you loosen up, reduce physical stress, and unwind with some simple, relaxing stretches.

When we stretch, we send a signal to our bodies to let go of the tension that builds up from sitting too long or being in high-stress situations. Stretching isn't just for athletes, it's for anyone who needs to feel a little lighter, calmer, and more at ease in their body.

Why Stretching Works: The Benefits of Loosening Up

Stretching does more than just make you feel good in the moment. It increases blood flow to your muscles, which helps them relax and recover. It also reduces muscle stiffness, improving your range of motion and flexibility. Regular stretching can even help lower stress hormones, making it an effective tool for reducing physical tension and emotional strain.

By incorporating stretching into your routine, you'll not only feel better physically, but you'll also enhance your overall sense of relaxation and well-being.

Step-by-Step: Simple Stretches for Tension Relief

Let's get started with some easy stretches to relieve tight muscles and reduce stress:

1. **Neck Stretch**: Sit or stand tall with your shoulders relaxed. Slowly tilt your head toward your right shoulder, bringing your ear toward it. Hold for 10-15 seconds, then slowly return to the center. Repeat on the left side. This helps release tension in your neck and shoulders.

2. **Shoulder Roll**: Stand or sit with your arms relaxed by your sides. Slowly roll your shoulders forward in a circular motion for 10 seconds, then reverse the direction for 10 seconds. This will loosen up tight shoulders and upper back muscles.

3. **Chest Stretch**: Stand tall and clasp your hands behind your back. Straighten your arms and gently lift them up, opening your chest. Hold for 15-20 seconds and breathe deeply. This helps release tension in the chest and improves posture.

4. **Hamstring Stretch**: Sit on the floor with one leg extended and the other bent. Reach for the toes of your extended leg, keeping your back straight. Hold for 20 seconds, then switch legs. This will stretch your hamstrings and relieve lower back tension.

5. **Seated Spinal Twist**: Sit with your legs extended in front of you. Cross one leg over the other, and twist your torso toward the bent leg. Hold for 15-20 seconds, then repeat on the other side. This helps loosen your lower back and spine.

6. **Child's Pose**: Kneel on the floor and slowly lower your body down toward your thighs, stretching your arms out in front of you. Hold for 30 seconds to a minute. This pose is great for calming the body and stretching the back.

Tracking Your Stretching Practice

What to Notice:

- Your stress level before and after (1-10 scale)
- Any tight or stiff areas you noticed before stretching
- Any changes in flexibility or mobility
- How long you held each stretch and how it felt
- Whether you noticed a difference in your mood or energy after stretching
- The best times of day for your stretching routine

Stretching Practice Log:

Date: _________ **Time:** _________ **Location:** _________________

Duration: _______________

Stress Level Before: 1-10______________________________

Stress Level After: 1-10________________________________

What I stretched: ____

What I noticed: ☐ Felt more relaxed ☐ Felt more flexible ☐ Felt more energized ☐ **Noticed relief in specific areas** ☐ Still felt some tightness ☐ Hard to focus on breathing

Best part of this session: ________________________________

What I'd change next time: ________________________________

Will I use this technique again? ☐ Definitely ☐ Maybe ☐ Probably not

Weekly Reflection:

After practicing for a week, what patterns do you notice? Which stretches are most helpful for you? Have you noticed improvements in your flexibility, tension relief, or stress reduction?

12

Listen to Music

Your Mood Reset Button

Have you ever felt out of balance, like everything is a bit too much, and then a song comes on that just *clicks*? Music has an incredible ability to reset our mood, shifting our emotional state in a matter of minutes. Whether you need to calm down after a stressful day or boost your energy for a big task, music can be the perfect companion to help you find your emotional footing. This chapter is all about using music as a tool to adjust your mood and energy. Whether it's a soothing melody to relax or an upbeat rhythm to get you moving, music holds the power to transform how you feel. Let's discuss how to harness this simple, yet powerful tool.

Why Music Works: The Emotional Power of Sound

Music is one of the most direct ways to influence our emotions. It's like a language that doesn't require words, it speaks directly to our brains and bodies. Research shows that music activates the same areas of the brain that respond to emotions, helping to regulate our feelings and energy levels. When we listen to music, it can help us calm down by lowering heart rates and relaxing our muscles. On the flip side, it can also energize us, making us feel more alert and motivated. In short, music can help us feel more in control of our emotions and our energy.

Step-by-Step: How to Use Music to Adjust Your Mood

Let's explore how to use music to reset your mood:

1. **Assess Your Mood**: Start by checking in with how you're feeling. Are you stressed, anxious, tired, or just in need of a mood boost? Understanding where you're at emotionally will help you choose the right kind of music.

2. **Choose the Right Music**: If you need to relax and de-stress, choose calming music—instrumental, classical, or even nature sounds. Slow tempos and gentle melodies are perfect for soothing your mind. If you need to boost your energy and motivation, go for upbeat, lively music; something with a strong rhythm that makes you want to move.

3. **Immerse Yourself**: Put on your headphones or play your chosen music out loud. Close your eyes if you can, and really focus on the sounds. Let the music fill you up, and let yourself be carried away by the rhythm or melody.

4. **Breathe and Let Go**: As you listen, pay attention to your body. Are you relaxing your shoulders? Are you breathing more deeply? Let the music do its work, whether it's calming you down or energizing you.

5. **Enjoy the Moment**: Allow yourself to enjoy the time you spend with the music. There's no rush. You're using this moment to reset your emotional state, so let it be a relaxing or uplifting experience.

Tracking Your Music Practice

What to Notice:

- Your stress or energy level before and after listening to music (1-

10 scale)

- Whether you felt more relaxed or energized
- The type of music that had the most effect on your mood
- Any physical sensations or emotional shifts
- How quickly the music impacted your mood
- The best times of day for using music to reset

Music Mood Reset Log:

Date: _________ **Time:** _________ **Location:** _________________

Duration: _________

Mood Before: ____________________ (1-10 scale)

Mood After: ____________________ (1-10 scale)

Music Genre/Type: ____

What I noticed: ☐ Felt more relaxed ☐ Felt more energized ☐ Felt more focused ☐ Felt happier ☐ Music made me reflect or calm down

Best part of this session: _____________________________________

What I'd change next time: __________________________________

Will I use this technique again? ☐ Definitely ☐ Maybe ☐ Probably not

Weekly Reflection:

After practicing for a week, what patterns do you notice? What kind of music works best for you in different situations? Have you found new songs or genres that really help adjust your mood?

13

Drink Water

Your Stress-Relief Hydration Strategy

It sounds so simple, doesn't it? Drink water. But there's more to it than just quenching your thirst; staying properly hydrated plays a key role in your emotional and physical well-being. We often underestimate how essential water is in managing stress, boosting energy, and maintaining mental clarity. This chapter is here to remind you how a simple glass of water can help reduce stress and bring your body back into balance. We've all experienced moments of feeling overwhelmed, tired, or mentally foggy. Often, it's because we're dehydrated, and our bodies and minds are struggling to function at their best. By making hydration a priority, you're giving your body the fuel it needs to stay calm, focused, and energized.

Why Drinking Water Works: The Science Behind Hydration

Water isn't just essential for physical health, it's crucial for emotional health, too. Dehydration can make you feel sluggish, irritable, and anxious. Studies show that even mild dehydration can impact your mood, energy levels, and ability to think clearly. On the other hand, staying well-hydrated helps maintain a balanced nervous system, reduces feelings of stress, and enhances focus.

Hydration also helps maintain the flow of oxygen and nutrients to your brain, which means your mind can stay sharp and clear. When you drink enough water, you're not only taking care of your body, but you're also taking care of your mental state.

Step-by-Step: How to Hydrate for Calm and Focus

Let's take a mindful approach to hydration with these simple steps:

1. **Choose Your Drink**: Grab a glass or bottle of water. If you prefer, you can infuse it with a slice of lemon, cucumber, or mint for a refreshing twist.

2. **Take It Slow**: Don't just gulp it down in one go. Sip slowly and focus on the process. Feel the coolness of the water as it passes your lips, and take a moment to appreciate the simple act of nourishing your body.

3. **Pay Attention**: Notice how your body feels as you drink. Are you feeling a little more refreshed? A little less tense? Drinking water can be a mindful experience that helps you reconnect with your body.

4. **Make It a Habit**: Try to drink water regularly throughout the day, not just when you're thirsty. Having a water bottle within reach can remind you to stay hydrated consistently.

Tracking Your Hydration Practice

What to Notice:

- Your stress level before and after drinking water (1-10 scale)
- How quickly you begin to feel more focused, energized, or calm
- Whether you noticed a shift in your mood after hydrating
- The types of situations where drinking water was most helpful for stress relief How your hydration habits impact your overall energy and mental clarity

Hydration Log:

Date: _________ **Time:** _________ **Location:** _________________

Duration: _________

Stress Level Before: 1-10____________________________

Stress Level After: 1-10______________________________

Amount of Water Drunk: ____________________________

What I noticed: ☐ Felt more energized ☐ Felt calmer ☐ Felt more focused ☐ Noticed less tension ☐ Felt a sense of relief

Best part of this session: ________________________________

What I'd change next time: ________________________________

Will I use this technique again? ☐ Definitely ☐ Maybe ☐ Probably not

Weekly Reflection:

After practicing for a week, what patterns do you notice? When is drinking water most helpful for reducing stress or increasing focus? How have your hydration habits impacted your overall mood and energy?

14

Eat a Snack Mindfully

Your Path to a Relaxed, Enjoyable Snack

In today's busy world, it's easy to rush through meals or snacks without really thinking about them. We might eat while working, watching TV, or scrolling through our phones, but have you ever paused to truly enjoy the experience of eating? Mindful eating invites you to slow down, focus on each bite, and truly connect with your body's natural hunger cues. This chapter will walk you through how to practice mindful eating to reduce stress, increase satisfaction, and even improve your digestion.

Mindful eating isn't about dieting or restrictive habits, it's about paying attention to how food makes you feel, savoring the flavors, and being present during your meals. By doing so, you'll naturally cultivate a deeper appreciation for food and feel more in tune with your body.

Why Mindful Eating Works: The Power of Presence

When we eat mindlessly, we often don't realize how much we're consuming, how it makes us feel, or whether we're truly hungry. Mindful eating helps us break this cycle by encouraging us to pay full attention to the act of eating, including the taste, texture, and smell of food. This practice can help reduce overeating, improve digestion, and foster a sense of relaxation and satisfaction.

Research shows that mindful eating can lead to improved digestion by promoting better chewing and slower eating, which aids in the body's ability to process food. It also helps reduce stress by encouraging a moment of pause, which calms the nervous system and allows you to focus on the present moment.

Step-by-Step: How to Eat a Snack Mindfully

Let's discuss how you can savor your next snack with mindfulness:

1. **Choose Your Snack**: Select a snack that you enjoy and that nourishes your body. It could be a handful of nuts, fruit, or anything you enjoy eating. The key is to pick something that you're excited to savor.

2. **Sit Down and Set the Scene**: Find a quiet spot to sit down, away from distractions. Take a moment to breathe deeply and relax. This helps you transition from a busy, rushed mindset into a more present, focused state.

3. **Engage Your Senses**: Before taking a bite, observe the food. Notice its colors, textures, and smells. Take a deep breath and appreciate the experience of having this snack.

4. **Eat Slowly**: Take your first bite, and focus entirely on the taste and texture. Chew slowly, savoring the flavors and the sensations in your mouth. Notice how the food feels, the sweetness, or the crunchiness.

5. **Listen to Your Body**: As you continue eating, pay attention to your body's cues. Are you feeling satisfied? Are you still hungry, or is your body asking for you to stop? Let your body guide the process.

6. **Finish with Gratitude**: Once you've finished, take a moment to reflect on how you feel. How did the snack make you feel physically and emotionally? Do you feel more relaxed or more energized? Ap-

preciate the nourishment you've given your body.

Tracking Your Mindful Eating Practice

What to Notice:

- Your stress level before and after eating (1-10 scale)
- The experience of eating slowly and savoring each bite
- How the food made you feel; physically and emotionally
- Whether you noticed any changes in your digestion or satisfaction
- How your body felt during and after the snack

Mindful Eating Log:

Date: _________ **Time:** _________ **Location:** _________________

Duration: _________

Stress Level Before: 1-10________________________________

Stress Level After: 1-10____________________________________

Snack I Ate: ____

____

What I noticed: ☐ Felt more relaxed ☐ Enjoyed the taste and texture ☐ Felt more satisfied ☐ Felt calmer ☐ Digestion was easier

Best part of this session: ________________________________

What I'd change next time: ________________________________

Will I use this technique again? ☐ Definitely ☐ Maybe ☐ Probably not

Weekly Reflection:

After practicing for a week, what patterns do you notice? How has mindful eating affected your stress levels, digestion, and enjoyment of food? Have you noticed any changes in your eating habits or how you approach meals and snacks?

15

Call or Text a Friend

Your Instant Mood Booster Through Connection

Sometimes, the best way to lift your spirits is by reaching out to someone you care about. Whether it's a quick text, a phone call, or even a video chat, connecting with a friend can provide emotional support, fresh perspective, and a sense of relief when stress feels overwhelming. In this chapter, we'll explore how taking a moment to connect with a loved one can be a simple, yet powerful, tool for reducing stress and boosting your mood.

We often forget how much power our social connections hold. In a world where we can feel isolated or overwhelmed by our own thoughts, just hearing a friendly voice or exchanging messages with someone who cares can make a world of difference. This chapter is about using those connections intentionally to improve your emotional well-being and foster positive relationships.

Why Reaching Out Works: The Science of Social Support

Humans are social creatures, and our brains are wired to seek out connection. Research shows that social support, whether through family, friends, or other loved ones, can lower levels of cortisol, the body's primary stress hormone. It also increases the production of oxytocin, a hormone associated with bonding and positive emotions. In other words, when you connect with others, your body receives a signal to relax and feel supported.

Socializing can also help us gain perspective. Sometimes, when we're stressed, we get caught up in our own thoughts and worries. Talking to a friend can help us see things from a different angle, offering reassurance and reminding us that we're not alone in what we're going through.

Step-by-Step: How to Reach Out and Reconnect

Let's walk through how to use your connections as a tool for stress relief:

1. **Choose a Friend**: Think of someone you trust, whether it's a close friend, family member, or even a colleague who has become a good friend over time. This person should be someone you feel comfortable with and who has a positive influence on your mood.

2. **Decide How to Reach Out**: Whether it's a phone call, a text message, or a quick chat on social media, choose the method that feels best for you in the moment.

3. **Send a Casual Message or Call**: Start with a simple greeting like, "*Hey, how's it going?*" or "*Got a minute to chat?*" It doesn't need to be deep or intense, just a way to open the door to a conversation.

4. **Chat and Listen**: Let the conversation flow naturally. Share how you're feeling if you'd like, or simply listen and enjoy catching up. The goal is to reconnect and offer each other support in whatever way feels right.

5. **End on a Positive Note**: When you finish your chat, notice how you feel. Do you feel lighter, more positive, or less stressed? Appreciate the connection you've made and how it's helped you shift your mood.

Tracking Your Social Connection Practice

What to Notice:

- Your stress level before and after connecting (1-10 scale)
- How the conversation impacted your mood and energy
- Whether the chat helped you gain perspective on any challenges
- How often you connect with others and whether it's making a difference in your stress levels
- The positive effects of socializing on your emotional well-being

Connection Log:

Date: _________ **Time:** _________ **Location:** _________________

Duration: _________

Stress Level Before: 1-10_________________________

Stress Level After: 1-10___________________________

How I Reached Out: ____________________________

What I noticed: ☐ Felt supported ☐ Gained perspective ☐ Felt lighter ☐ Felt more connected ☐ Felt more relaxed ☐ Enjoyed the conversation

Best part of this session: ________________________________

What I'd change next time: ________________________________

Will I use this technique again? ☐ Definitely ☐ Maybe ☐ Probably not

Weekly Reflection:

After practicing for a week, what patterns do you notice? When is connecting with friends most helpful for you? How has it impacted your overall mood and stress levels? What adjustments have you made to make these connections more fulfilling?

16

Try Aromatherapy

Your Sensory Escape to Calmness

In moments of stress or overwhelm, it's amazing how a simple scent can help bring you back to a place of peace. Aromatherapy is a powerful tool that taps into your sense of smell to soothe your mind and relax your body. Whether it's the calming scent of lavender or the refreshing aroma of peppermint, certain smells have the ability to influence our emotions and reduce stress. In this chapter, we'll explore how essential oils and candles can enhance relaxation and bring balance to your day.

Aromatherapy is more than just a pleasant fragrance; it's a way to tap into the body's natural ability to relax. By incorporating aromatherapy into your routine, you can create a soothing environment that helps calm your mind, improve your sleep, and elevate your mood.

Why Aromatherapy Works: The Science of Scent and Relaxation

The power of aromatherapy lies in its ability to influence the brain through the olfactory system. When you inhale a scent, molecules from the fragrance enter the nose and stimulate the limbic system, the part of the brain responsible for emotions and memory. This triggers physiological responses, such as reduced heart rate, lowered blood pressure, and a calmer state of mind.

Certain essential oils, like lavender and chamomile, have been shown to reduce anxiety and improve sleep quality, while uplifting scents like citrus or peppermint can energize and clear the mind. Whether you need to unwind after a long day or need a quick mood boost, aromatherapy offers a simple and effective way to enhance your emotional well-being.

Step-by-Step: How to Use Aromatherapy for Stress Relief

Let's walk through how to incorporate aromatherapy into your routine to soothe your senses:

1. **Choose Your Essential Oils or Scented Candles**: Select a scent based on your needs:

    - For relaxation and stress relief, try lavender, chamomile, or sandalwood.
    - For mental clarity and focus, opt for peppermint, rosemary, or citrus scents like orange or lemon.
    - For a mood boost, go for uplifting scents like eucalyptus, bergamot, or jasmine.

2. **Set the Scene**: Find a quiet space where you can relax. Dim the lights, sit comfortably, and prepare your chosen scent.

3. **Use Essential Oils**: If you're using essential oils, you can add a few drops to a diffuser or dilute them with a carrier oil and apply them to pulse points like your wrists or temples. Breathe in deeply and allow the aroma to fill your space.

4. **Light a Candle**: If you prefer candles, light one and place it in a space

where you can easily inhale the scent. Let the soft flicker of the flame add to the calming atmosphere.

5. **Breathe and Relax**: Close your eyes, take a few deep breaths, and focus on the scent. Allow yourself to fully relax into the moment. Let the aroma soothe your mind, calm your nervous system, and create a peaceful environment.

6. **Enjoy the Moment**: Stay with the scent for at least 10-15 minutes. The goal is to truly savor the experience, letting the fragrance take you into a more relaxed state.

Tracking Your Aromatherapy Practice

What to Notice:

- Your stress level before and after using aromatherapy (1-10 scale)
- How the scent made you feel; more relaxed, energized, or focused
- Whether the scent helped reduce anxiety or improved your mood
- How quickly you felt the calming effects
- The best times of day to use aromatherapy

Aromatherapy Log:

Date: _________ **Time:** _________ **Location:** _________________

Duration: _________

Stress Level Before: 1-10______________________________

Stress Level After: 1-10________________________________

Scent Used: ____

What I noticed: ☐ Felt more relaxed ☐ Felt more focused ☐ Mood improved ☐ Anxiety reduced ☐ Scent helped with sleep ☐ Felt energized

Best part of this session: ________________________________

What I'd change next time: ________________________________

Will I use this technique again? ☐ Definitely ☐ Maybe ☐ Probably not

Weekly Reflection:

After practicing for a week, what patterns do you notice? Which scents are most helpful for you? Have you noticed a shift in your mood, anxiety levels, or sleep quality after using aromatherapy?

17

Name Your Emotions

Your Path to Emotional Clarity

It's easy to get caught up in the swirl of emotions and feel overwhelmed by what's happening inside. Sometimes, emotions can feel so big that we don't know where to start. But what if you could step back for a moment and simply name what you're feeling? Identifying and naming your emotions is a simple yet powerful technique that can help you regain clarity, control, and a healthier way to process what's going on inside. In this chapter, we'll explore how this practice promotes emotional awareness and makes it easier to handle your emotions in a mindful way.

Naming your emotions doesn't mean overthinking or labeling yourself with one feeling forever, it's about giving a name to the emotion you're experiencing, which helps you gain perspective. Once you label your emotions, you create space to respond thoughtfully instead of reacting impulsively.

Why Naming Emotions Works: The Power of Understanding

Emotions can sometimes feel like they're taking over, but when we put a name to what we're feeling, we begin to separate ourselves from the emotion. Research shows that simply identifying and labeling our feelings can reduce their intensity and help us gain control over them. When we don't recognize our emotions, they can become overwhelming, but by acknowledging them, we can address them in a healthier way.

By naming our emotions, we increase our emotional intelligence and awareness, allowing us to understand our triggers, express ourselves better, and navigate our feelings with greater ease. This practice helps us improve emotional regulation and respond to situations more mindfully.

Step-by-Step: How to Name Your Emotions

Here's how to start identifying and naming your feelings:

1. **Pause and Check In**: When you're feeling overwhelmed or stressed, take a moment to pause. Close your eyes if you can, and focus on your breath. This helps you settle into the present moment.

2. **Observe Your Feelings**: Pay attention to what's happening inside. Are you feeling anxious, frustrated, sad, or excited? Are there physical sensations in your body that point to a specific emotion, like a tight chest, clenched jaw, or fluttering stomach?

3. **Name the Emotion**: Once you've identified how you're feeling, give that emotion a name. Is it anxiety, anger, disappointment, joy, or something else? You might feel a mix of emotions, and that's okay, try to name the dominant feeling.

4. **Acknowledge the Emotion**: Once you've named it, acknowledge it without judgment. Allow yourself to feel whatever you're feeling, but remember, naming it gives you power over it.

5. **Ask Yourself Why**: If you're up for it, ask yourself why you feel this way. What triggered this emotion? Understanding the root cause can offer valuable insights into your emotional state.

Tracking Your Emotional Awareness Practice

What to Notice:

- Your stress level before and after naming your emotions (1-10 scale)
- Whether naming the emotion made it easier to process or release
- How recognizing the emotion impacted your reactions
- Whether naming your emotions helped you respond more mindfully
- How often you name your emotions and any patterns that emerge

Emotional Awareness Log:

Date: ________ **Time:** ________ **Location:** _______________

Duration: ________

Stress Level Before: 1-10____________________

Stress Level After: 1-10_____________________

Emotion I Felt: ______________________________________

What I noticed:

☐ Felt more in control ☐ Easier to express my feelings ☐ Reduced intensity of the emotion ☐ Felt more aware of what triggered me

Best part of this session: ____________________________

What I'd change next time: ____________________________

Will I use this technique again? ☐ Definitely ☐ Maybe ☐ Probably not

Weekly Reflection:

After practicing for a week, what patterns do you notice? How has naming your emotions helped you manage stress? Are there specific emotions you tend to avoid or struggle with? How has this practice impacted your emotional clarity and responses?

18

Visualization

Your Mental Escape to Calmness

Imagine this: You're lying on a warm beach, the sound of gentle waves lapping against the shore, a soft breeze brushing your skin. You can feel the warmth of the sun and the peace of the surroundings. As you sit back and breathe deeply, all your worries seem to fade into the distance. Visualization works like that by mentally transporting yourself to a peaceful place, you can reduce stress, find mental clarity, and reset your emotional state. In this chapter, we'll explore how guided imagery can be your ticket to relaxation and a calmer mind.

Visualization isn't just about escaping reality; it's about giving yourself the space to breathe and recharge. By using your imagination to create calming scenes, you can tap into the power of your mind to reduce tension, clear away mental fog, and boost emotional well-being. It's a simple practice that can offer big rewards, especially when stress is high.

Why Visualization Works: The Power of Your Imagination

Visualization is a powerful tool because it directly taps into your body's stress-response system. When you imagine yourself in a peaceful, relaxing place, your body responds as though you're actually there. Your heart rate slows, your breathing deepens, and the tension you've been carrying melts away. Studies show that guided imagery can lower stress levels, improve mood, and even enhance your ability to focus. By regularly practicing visualization, you can create a sense of calm that stays with you even after the session ends.

The beauty of visualization is that it's a portable, accessible technique; you can use it anywhere, anytime, to take a quick mental break from life's demands. Whether you need to de-stress during a busy workday or wind down before bed, visualization offers a soothing and effective solution.

Step-by-Step: How to Use Visualization for Stress Relief

Let's walk through the process of visualization together:

1. **Find a Comfortable Spot**: Sit or lie down in a quiet, comfortable space where you won't be disturbed. Close your eyes, take a few deep breaths, and begin to relax.

2. **Create Your Peaceful Place**: Picture a place that makes you feel calm and at ease. It could be a beach, a forest, a mountaintop, or anywhere that feels peaceful to you. Imagine every detail; the colors, sounds, textures, and smells of this place.

3. **Engage Your Senses**: The more vivid and detailed your visualization, the more powerful it will be. Focus on how the air feels against your skin, the sounds of nature around you, and any other sensations that make this place feel real. Really immerse yourself in the experience.

4. **Breathe and Relax**: As you visualize, take slow, deep breaths. Let the peacefulness of your imagined environment fill your mind and

body. With each breath, allow your muscles to relax even more deeply.

5. **Stay as Long as You Need**: You can stay in this peaceful place for as long as you like. If your mind begins to wander, gently bring your focus back to the details of your visualization. Let the calmness envelop you fully.

6. **Finish Slowly**: When you're ready, slowly bring your focus back to the present. Take a few moments to reflect on how your body and mind feel. Notice any shift in tension or stress.

Tracking Your Visualization Practice

What to Notice:

- Your stress level before and after visualizing (1-10 scale)
- How vivid and detailed your visualization was
- How your body responded (did you feel more relaxed, less tense, etc.)
- Whether visualization helped improve your mood or mental clarity
- The types of environments that worked best for you

Visualization Log:

Date: ____________ **Time:** _________ **Location:** _________________

Duration: _________

Stress Level Before: 1-10____________________

Stress Level After: 1-10______________________

Environment Visualized: ____________________________________

What I noticed: ☐ Felt more relaxed ☐ Felt more focused ☐ Felt clearer mentally ☐ Was able to release tension ☐ Was able to let go of worries

Best part of this session: ________________________________

What I'd change next time: __________________________________

____

Will I use this technique again?

☐ Definitely ☐ Maybe ☐ Probably not

Weekly Reflection:

After practicing for a week, what patterns do you notice? Which visualizations work best for you? Have you noticed any changes in your stress levels, mood, or clarity? How has visualization impacted your ability to cope with stress?

19

Do a Puzzle or Game

Your Stress-Free Mind Break

Sometimes, the best way to deal with stress is to give your mind something else to focus on. When you're feeling overwhelmed, engaging in a puzzle or game can help distract you from stress and give your brain a well-deserved break. In this chapter, we'll explore how activities like puzzles, board games, or brain teasers can provide mental relief and help you shift focus away from stress.

It might seem counterintuitive, why would something like a game or a puzzle help reduce stress? But the truth is, these activities force your mind to focus on something else. They help clear your mental clutter and give you the chance to reset. Plus, the sense of accomplishment you feel when you finish a puzzle or win a game can give you an instant mood boost.

Why Puzzles and Games Work: The Power of Distraction

Puzzles and games provide a fun, interactive way to distract your mind from worries and stress. They work because they require full attention, which means your brain is focused on the task at hand rather than on your anxiety or tension. This shift in focus gives you a mental break, allowing your stress levels to lower. Additionally, engaging in these activities can improve cognitive function by boosting memory, problem-solving skills, and attention. When you're focusing on a puzzle or a game, your brain is exercising in a way that helps sharpen your thinking and improve your overall mental clarity.

Step-by-Step: How to Use a Puzzle or Game to Relieve Stress

Let's walk through the process of using a puzzle or game to take a mental break:

1. **Choose Your Activity**: Whether it's a jigsaw puzzle, sudoku, crossword, or a mobile game, pick something that interests you and is engaging but not too overwhelming.

2. **Set Up Your Space**: Find a quiet space where you can focus without distractions. Gather your materials; your puzzle pieces, board game, or app, and get comfortable.

3. **Engage and Focus**: Begin the puzzle or game, giving your full attention to the task. As you work through it, let yourself get lost in the activity. Forget about everything else, this is your time to focus solely on the puzzle or game.

4. **Enjoy the Process**: While solving the puzzle or playing the game, focus on how your mind is shifting away from stress. Notice how you feel as you focus on one piece at a time or progress through levels.

5. **Celebrate Your Achievement**: Whether you finish a puzzle or complete a game, take a moment to celebrate your progress. Completing a task, no matter how small, boosts your mood and gives you a sense of accomplishment.

Tracking Your Puzzle or Game Practice

What to Notice:

- Your stress level before and after engaging in the activity (1-10 scale)
- How focused you were during the game or puzzle
- Whether you felt less stressed or more relaxed after the activity
- How long it took you to finish the activity
- The mental clarity or energy boost you felt after completing it
- The types of puzzles or games that work best for you

Puzzle or Game Log:

Date: _________ **Time:** _________ **Location:** _________________

Duration: _________

Stress Level Before: 1-10_____________________

Stress Level After: 1-10______________________

Activity Type: ____

What I noticed:

☐ Felt more relaxed ☐ Felt more focused ☐ Enjoyed the distraction ☐ Felt mentally sharper ☐ Felt a sense of accomplishment

Best part of this session: ________________________________

What I'd change next time: ________________________________

Will I use this technique again? ☐ Definitely ☐ Maybe ☐ Probably not

Weekly Reflection:

After practicing for a week, what patterns do you notice? Which puzzles or games are most effective for distracting you from stress? How has this practice impacted your focus, mental clarity, or mood?

20

Take a Power Nap

Your Quick Recharge for Mind and Body

When was the last time you felt completely drained, like your energy was running on empty? We often push ourselves through the day without giving our bodies the rest they crave. But what if I told you that just a short nap could be the perfect solution to recharge your energy, boost your mood, and improve your focus? This chapter will guide you through the benefits of power naps, and why taking a 10-20 minute nap can be an incredibly effective stress-relief tool. A power nap isn't about sleeping for hours, it's about giving your body and mind a quick reset. It's like pressing a refresh button that leaves you feeling more alert, focused, and ready to tackle whatever comes next.

Why Power Naps Work: The Science of Quick Rest

Power naps work wonders because they tap into the natural sleep cycle without entering deep sleep. This means you can feel refreshed without the grogginess that comes from longer naps. Research shows that a short nap (10-20 minutes) can enhance focus, improve mood, and increase alertness helping you feel recharged without wasting time.

Napping allows your brain to process information and recharge your mental batteries. It also helps lower stress levels and boost productivity. In short, a quick nap provides a much-needed break for both your mind and body, making it a powerful tool for combating fatigue and stress.

Step-by-Step: How to Take a Power Nap

Let's walk through how you can maximize the benefits of a power nap:

1. **Set a Timer**: Decide on the perfect nap duration, 10 to 20 minutes. Set an alarm to avoid oversleeping and feeling groggy.

2. **Find a Comfortable Spot**: Choose a quiet, comfortable place where you can lie down or rest without distractions. Make sure it's dark or dimly lit to help signal to your body that it's time to rest.

3. **Close Your Eyes and Relax**: Take a few deep breaths and let go of any tension. Don't stress about falling asleep, just allow yourself to rest and relax.

4. **Focus on Breathing**: If your mind starts to race, focus on your breath. Take slow, deep breaths to calm your thoughts and help you drift into a restful state.

5. **Wake Up Gently**: Once your timer goes off, gently bring your awareness back to the present. Take a few moments to stretch and notice how you feel. Ideally, you'll feel refreshed, not groggy, and ready to get back to your day.

Tracking Your Power Nap Practice

What to Notice:

- Your energy level before and after the nap (1-10 scale)
- How quickly you fall asleep and how deeply you rest

- Any improvement in focus, mood, or alertness after waking
- Whether you feel groggy or refreshed after the nap
- The best times of day for you to take a power nap

Power Nap Log:

Date: _________ **Time:** _________ **Location:** ____________________

Duration: __________

Energy Level Before: 1-10___________________

Energy Level After: 1-10____________________

Mood Before: ____________________ (1-10 scale)

Mood After: ____________________ (1-10 scale)

What I noticed: ☐ Felt more focused ☐ Felt more energized ☐ Felt more alert ☐ Felt less stressed ☐ Didn't feel groggy

Best part of this session: ________________________________

What I'd change next time: ________________________________

Will I use this technique again? ☐ Definitely ☐ Maybe ☑Probably not

Weekly Reflection:

After practicing for a week, what patterns do you notice? When is the best time for you to take a power nap? How has napping impacted your energy levels, focus, and mood throughout the day?

21

Repeat a Mantra

Your Tool for Rewiring Negative Thoughts

We all have those moments when negative thoughts seem to take over. Whether it's a self-doubt that keeps resurfacing or a feeling of stress that just won't let go, our minds can get stuck in unproductive thought patterns. But what if you had a tool that could help you shift your thinking and break free from negativity? Repeating a mantra can be a powerful way to rewire your brain, replacing those negative thoughts with empowering, positive affirmations. In this chapter, we'll explore how mantras can help you build emotional resilience, shift your mindset, and reclaim your peace.

A mantra is more than just a word or phrase, it's a reminder of who you are and the positive energy you want to cultivate. When repeated with intention, mantras can change your emotional state and even help you manage stress more effectively.

Why Repeating a Mantra Works: The Science of Positive Affirmations

Mantras work by helping you refocus your mind. When we repeat a positive phrase, we interrupt the flow of negative or stressful thoughts and create new neural pathways in the brain. Essentially, the more you repeat a positive affirmation, the stronger that belief becomes in your mind.

Research shows that repeating mantras can significantly reduce stress and anxiety, improve mood, and even increase feelings of self-compassion. By focusing on a calming or empowering phrase, you shift your attention away from stress and toward a more positive, resilient mindset.

Step-by-Step: How to Use a Mantra for Stress Relief

Let's discuss how you can incorporate mantra repetition into your routine:

1. **Choose Your Mantra**: Pick a mantra that resonates with you; something short, simple, and positive. It could be something like "*I am enough,*" "*I am calm,*" "*I am strong,*" or "*This too shall pass.*" The key is that it should feel empowering and relevant to what you need in the moment.

2. **Find a Quiet Space**: Sit or lie down in a comfortable position where you can focus. Close your eyes and take a deep breath to center yourself.

3. **Repeat Your Mantra**: Begin repeating your chosen mantra silently or aloud. Focus on the words and let them fill your mind. With each repetition, feel the power of those words grounding you.

4. **Breathe and Relax**: As you continue to repeat your mantra, breathe slowly and deeply. Let your body relax with each exhale, and allow the mantra to calm your thoughts.

5. **Stay with It**: Continue repeating the mantra for several minutes. If your mind starts to wander, gently bring it back to the words you're saying. This is about creating a mental space that's focused and peaceful.

6. **Finish with Gratitude**: When you're done, take a moment to reflect on how you feel. Do you feel more relaxed? More focused? Notice any shift in your emotional state?

Tracking Your Mantra Practice

What to Notice:

- Your stress level before and after repeating the mantra (1-10 scale)
- Whether repeating the mantra helped quiet your mind or shift your focus
- The emotional or physical sensations you experienced
- How often you practice your mantra and its impact on your daily stress
- The best times of day to repeat your mantra

Mantra Log

Date: _________ **Time:** _________ **Location:** _________________

Duration: _________

Stress Level Before: 1-10______________________

Stress Level After: 1-10_______________________

Mantra Used: ____

What I noticed: ☐ Felt more calm ☐ Felt more focused ☐ Shifted my perspective ☐ Reduced anxiety ☐ Felt more confident

Best part of this session: ________________________________

What I'd change next time: ________________________________

Will I use this technique again? ☐ Definitely ☐ Maybe ☐ Probably not

Weekly Reflection:
After practicing for a week, what patterns do you notice? How has repeating mantras affected your stress, mood, and emotional resilience? Have you found certain mantras to be more effective than others? How has this practice shifted your perspective on challenges?

22

Declutter a Tiny Space

Your Quick Path to a Calmer Environment

Ever feel like your surroundings are cluttered, and it's making your mind feel the same way? It's no surprise, our physical environment often mirrors our mental state. When we're surrounded by chaos or disorganization, it can leave us feeling overwhelmed and stressed. But the good news is that you don't need to overhaul your entire home to experience relief. Sometimes, all it takes is decluttering a small space, like your desk or a drawer, to create a sense of calm and accomplishment. This chapter will guide you through how tidying up just one area can reduce stress and bring clarity to your day.

Decluttering isn't just about tidying up, it's a stress-relief technique that helps you regain control over your environment, which in turn helps you feel more in control of your thoughts and emotions. By clearing out the physical clutter, you also clear mental clutter, allowing you to focus and relax more easily.

Why Decluttering Works: The Psychology of a Tidy Space

Decluttering has a profound impact on our mental health. Research shows that when we're surrounded by clutter, our brains are constantly processing the mess, which can lead to increased stress and anxiety. On the flip side, organizing a small area creates a sense of order, which helps calm the mind and improve focus. It also gives you a sense of accomplishment, reinforcing positive emotions and reducing feelings of overwhelm.

A tidy space helps reduce distractions, making it easier to concentrate and think clearly. When you take a few minutes to declutter, you create an environment that supports relaxation and productivity, which is a great foundation for managing stress.

Step-by-Step: How to Declutter a Tiny Space

Let's discuss the process of decluttering one small area, such as your desk, a drawer, or a shelf:

1. **Pick Your Space**: Choose a small, manageable area to start with. It could be your desk, a single drawer, or even a corner of a room. The key is to keep it simple and not too overwhelming.

2. **Set a Timer**: Give yourself a time limit to avoid getting lost in the task. A 10-20 minute timer is perfect to keep you focused without it feeling like a chore.

3. **Sort and Purge**: Take everything out of the space and sort through the items. Ask yourself if you really need each thing. If it's something you haven't used in months or it doesn't bring you joy, consider letting it go. Donate or recycle items that no longer serve you.

4. **Organize**: Once you've removed the unnecessary items, arrange the things you're keeping in a way that feels tidy and functional. Group similar items together, and make sure everything has a designated place.

5. **Clean the Area**: Wipe down surfaces and refresh the space. A clean environment will contribute to a clearer mind and a greater sense of calm.

6. **Enjoy the Space**: Take a moment to appreciate how much better the space looks and how you feel. The sense of accomplishment and the new calmness in your environment will help shift your mood and reduce stress.

Tracking Your Decluttering Practice

What to Notice:

- Your stress level before and after decluttering (1-10 scale)
- How your mood changes as you organize
- Whether organizing the space helped improve your focus or mental clarity
- How the decluttered space impacts your overall sense of calm and well-being
- Whether you feel more in control of your environment

Declutter Log:

Date: _________ **Time:** _________ **Location:** _________________

Duration: _________

Stress Level Before: 1-10_________________________

Stress Level After: 1-10__________________________

Space Decluttered: ____

What I noticed: ☐ Felt more organized ☐ Felt calmer ☐ Felt accomplished ☐ Environment felt more peaceful ☐ Improved focus and productivity

Best part of this session: _____________________________________

____

What I'd change next time: ________________________________

Will I use this technique again? ☐ Definitely ☐ Maybe ☐ Probably not

Weekly Reflection:

After practicing for a week, what patterns do you notice? How has decluttering impacted your stress levels, focus, and mood? Are there any specific spaces in your home that are more beneficial to declutter for stress relief?

23

Laugh

Your Instant Stress-Buster

When was the last time you had a good laugh that made your whole body feel lighter? Laughter is one of the simplest and most effective ways to relieve stress. It's not just about cracking jokes or watching a funny video, it's about how humor can instantly shift your mood and help you escape the weight of tension. This chapter is all about showing you how to incorporate laughter into your routine as a tool for improving your mood and reducing stress.

Laughter is a natural stress reliever that provides a powerful antidote to anxiety and overwhelm. When you laugh, your body releases endorphins, those feel-good chemicals that improve your mood and boost your sense of well-being. It's an instant way to lighten up and break free from the emotional heaviness of stress.

Why Laughter Works: The Science of Humor

Laughter has an immediate impact on your body. When you laugh, your muscles relax, your heart rate slows, and your body's stress hormones decrease. This relaxation effect makes laughter a powerful tool for stress relief and mental clarity. But it's not just about physical relaxation, laughter also activates the brain's reward centers, promoting a positive mental state and making you feel more optimistic and energized.

Moreover, laughter can help shift your perspective, making challenges feel more manageable. It helps you take a step back, stop taking things too seriously, and see the humor in difficult situations. Plus, laughter is contagious! When you laugh, you invite others to laugh with you, creating an uplifting atmosphere for everyone involved.

Step-by-Step: How to Incorporate Laughter into Your Routine

Let's walk through a few ways you can bring more laughter into your day:

1. **Watch Something Funny**: Put on a comedy show, a funny movie, or a YouTube video that always makes you laugh. Whether it's stand-up comedy, funny animal videos, or your favorite sitcom, choose something that lifts your spirits and makes you smile.

2. **Recall a Humorous Memory**: Think of a funny moment from your past—maybe a silly thing that happened with friends or a hilarious childhood memory. As you recall the moment, let yourself laugh at the memory and relive the joy it brought you.

3. **Listen to a Comedy Podcast or Radio Show**: If you don't have time to watch something, listen to a comedy podcast while you're on the go. Laughter doesn't require a screen; sometimes, all you need is a funny conversation or story to boost your mood.

4. **Laugh with Friends**: Call or text a friend who always makes you laugh. Sometimes, a quick chat with someone who has a great sense of humor can instantly lift your mood.

5. **Laugh on Purpose**: If you're feeling stressed and need a quick reset, try laughing intentionally. Even if you don't feel like it, just

starting with a fake laugh can trigger a real one. It sounds silly, but it works!

Tracking Your Laughter Sessions

What to Notice:

- Your stress level before and after laughing (1-10 scale)
- How your mood shifted after laughing
- Whether you felt more relaxed or energized
- The types of humor or content that made you laugh the most
- How laughter impacted your perspective or ability to cope with stress

Laughter Log:

Date: _________ **Time:** _________ **Location:** _________________

Duration: _________

Stress Level Before: 1-10_________________________

Stress Level After: 1-10__________________________

What Made Me Laugh: _____________________________________

What I noticed: ☐ Felt more relaxed ☐ Felt more energized ☐ Mood improved ☐ Perspective shifted ☐ Laughter made stress feel more manageable

Best part of this session: ________________________________

What I'd change next time: ________________________________

Will I use this technique again? ☐ Definitely ☐ Maybe ☐ Probably not

Weekly Reflection:

After practicing for a week, what patterns do you notice? When does laughter have the most positive effect on your stress levels? How has it impacted your ability to cope with challenges or shift your mood?

24

Practice Saying "No"

Your Tool for Protecting Your Time and Energy

How often do you say "*yes*" to things you don't really want to do? It's easy to fall into the habit of overcommitting, trying to please others, or taking on more than you can handle. But here's the truth: learning to say "*no*" is one of the most powerful self-care skills you can develop. In this chapter, we'll explore how setting healthy boundaries by saying "*no*" can protect your time, energy, and emotional well-being.

Saying "*no*" isn't about being selfish, it's about knowing your limits and respecting your needs. When you say "*no,*" you're giving yourself permission to prioritize your own well-being, which ultimately helps you be more present, focused, and emotionally healthy. The ability to say "*no*" is crucial for reducing stress, preventing burnout, and maintaining balance in your life.

Why Saying "No" Works: The Power of Boundaries

Setting boundaries, including learning to say "*no,*" is essential for protecting your emotional health. When we say "*yes*" too often, we can end up overwhelmed, drained, and resentful. Saying "*no*" allows us to regain control over our time and energy, helping us focus on what truly matters. It's an empowering choice that promotes respect for ourselves and our needs.

Studies show that people who set clear boundaries experience lower levels of stress and burnout. By honoring our limits, we're not just protecting our time, we're also protecting our mental and emotional well-being. Saying "*no*" doesn't make us bad or unkind; it makes us wise and self-aware.

Step-by-Step: How to Practice Saying "No" Without Guilt

Let's walk through how you can practice saying "*no*" in a healthy, guilt-free way:

1. **Recognize Your Limits**: Before agreeing to anything, take a moment to check in with yourself. Are you already stretched too thin? Do you have the time, energy, and emotional capacity to take on more? If the answer is "*no,*" then it's time to set a boundary.

2. **Be Honest and Direct**: When you need to say "*no,*" keep it simple and clear. You don't need to over-explain yourself. A straightforward, "I'm unable to do that right now" is often all you need to say.

3. **Practice Self-Compassion**: It's natural to feel guilty when saying "*no,*" especially if you're used to pleasing others. But remind yourself that saying "*no*" is an act of self-care. You're not responsible for everyone else's happiness, and you deserve to protect your time and energy.

4. **Offer Alternatives (If Appropriate)**: If you feel comfortable, you can offer an alternative or compromise. For example, "*I can't help with that today, but maybe I can assist next week*" or "I*'m unable to commit right now, but I appreciate you thinking of me.*"

5. **Stick to Your Decision**: Once you've said "*no,*" trust your choice

and don't second-guess yourself. It's okay to decline an invitation or request, and it's okay to put yourself first when necessary.

Tracking Your "No" Practice

What to Notice:

- Your stress level before and after saying "no" (1-10 scale)
- How your mood shifted after setting a boundary
- Whether you experienced any guilt, and how you handled it
- The positive impact of saying "no" on your energy and time management
- How saying "no" helped you protect your emotional well-being

"No" Log:

Date: _________ **Time:** _________ **Location:** _________________

Duration: _________

Stress Level Before: 1-10__________________

Stress Level After: 1-10____________________

What I Said "No" To: _______________________________________

What I noticed: ☐ Felt empowered ☐ Felt more in control ☐ Less stressed ☐ Reduced sense of overwhelm ☐ Didn't feel guilty ☐ Protected my time and energy

Best part of this session: ________________________________

What I'd change next time: ________________________________

Will I use this technique again? ☐ Definitely ☐ Maybe ☐ Probably not

Weekly Reflection:

After practicing for a week, what patterns do you notice? How did saying "*no*" impact your stress levels, mood, and overall emotional health? Were there any situations where saying "*no*" felt particularly empowering or difficult?

25

Pet an Animal

Your Instant Source of Calm and Joy

There's something magical about spending time with animals, isn't there? Whether it's the soothing purr of a cat, the gentle nudge of a dog, or simply watching a pet curl up contentedly, animals have a unique ability to reduce stress and bring joy. This chapter introduces pet therapy as a powerful form of relaxation and self-care that can help you feel more grounded, calm, and connected.

Pets offer a comforting presence and unconditional love that can melt away stress. When we interact with animals, it's not just a pleasant distraction; it's a genuine emotional boost. Whether you have a pet of your own or spend time with animals in other ways, their calming influence can help soothe your soul and promote a more peaceful, joyful mindset.

Why Interacting with Animals Works: The Science Behind Pet Therapy

The benefits of interacting with animals go beyond the warm, fuzzy feelings they give us. Studies show that spending time with pets can lower cortisol (the stress hormone), reduce blood pressure, and increase the production of oxytocin, a hormone associated with bonding and happiness.

This combination of physical benefits makes pet therapy an excellent tool for improving emotional well-being.

When you pet or cuddle an animal, your body relaxes, your mood improves, and your stress levels drop. Even just watching an animal be content can have a soothing effect on your nervous system. This makes spending time with pets one of the easiest ways to reduce tension and boost happiness.

Step-by-Step: How to Spend Time with an Animal to Soothe Your Soul

Let's explore how you can make the most of your time with a pet:

1. **Find Your Pet or Animal**: If you have a pet, start by spending some time with them. If you don't, consider visiting a local animal shelter, a friend's pet, or even spending time with a stuffed animal if that's more accessible.

2. **Be Present with the Animal**: Focus on the experience of being with the animal. Pet them gently, watch their movements, and notice their calming effect. Let yourself enjoy the moment without distractions.

3. **Pay Attention to Your Body**: As you pet the animal, notice how your body reacts. Do your shoulders drop? Does your breathing slow down? These are signs that your body is relaxing.

4. **Engage with Play or Cuddling**: If the animal enjoys playtime, engage with them in a fun activity like fetching a toy or petting them in a way they enjoy. Playfulness can enhance the mood-boosting effects of your interaction.

5. **Appreciate the Bond**: Take a moment to appreciate the connection you share with the animal, whether it's your own pet or one you're spending time with. This bond can be incredibly therapeutic, providing both relax-

ation and emotional comfort.

Tracking Your Pet Therapy Practice

What to Notice:

- Your stress level before and after spending time with the animal (1-10 scale)
- Any physical relaxation you notice (e.g., slower heart rate, relaxed muscles)
- How your mood shifts after interacting with the animal
- Whether the animal's presence helps you feel more grounded or joyful
- The impact of regular animal interactions on your overall stress levels

Pet Interaction Log:

Date: _________ **Time:** _________ **Location:** _________________

Duration: _________

Stress Level Before: 1-10_________________________

Stress Level After: 1-10__________________________

Animal Interacted With: _____________________________________

What I noticed: ☐ Felt more relaxed ☐ Mood improved ☐ Felt calmer ☐ Enjoyed the connection ☐ Reduced anxiety

Best part of this session: ________________________________

What I'd change next time: ________________________________

Will I use this technique again? ☐ Definitely ☐ Maybe ☐ Probably not

Weekly Reflection:
After practicing for a week, what patterns do you notice? How does interacting with animals impact your stress levels, mood, and emotional health? How often do you find yourself reaching for the company of an animal to soothe your soul?

26

Try a Grounding Object

Your Tool for Staying Present

In the middle of a busy, stressful moment, it can feel like your emotions are spiraling out of control. Your mind races, and you're overwhelmed by what's happening around you. That's where grounding techniques come in. Grounding helps you reconnect with the present moment, easing feelings of anxiety and bringing a sense of calm. In this chapter, we'll explore how using a grounding object can help you stay centered and regain emotional balance.

A grounding object is a simple item, like a stone, coin, or any small object, that you use to focus your attention on the here and now. By turning your attention to the physical sensation of the object, you can anchor yourself in the present, shifting away from overwhelming emotions and stressful thoughts.

Why Grounding Works: The Power of the Present Moment

When we feel anxious or overwhelmed, our minds often race ahead, thinking about future worries or past regrets. Grounding techniques help break this cycle by bringing us back to the present moment, where we can feel more in control. Research shows that grounding exercises can significantly reduce anxiety, improve emotional regulation, and help people cope with stress in a more balanced way.

Using a grounding object works by redirecting your focus. By holding or focusing on an object, you create a sensory experience that helps shift your attention away from negative thoughts and back to the physical world around you. This simple act of mindfulness can create instant relief, helping you feel calmer and more centered.

Step-by-Step: How to Use a Grounding Object for Emotional Balance

Let's walk through the process of using a grounding object:

1. **Choose Your Object**: Find a small object that feels calming or interesting to you. This could be a smooth stone, a coin, a piece of jewelry, or any item you can easily hold in your hand.

2. **Get Comfortable**: Sit or stand in a comfortable position where you can focus. Take a few deep breaths to center yourself.

3. **Focus on the Object**: Hold the object in your hand and give it your full attention. Notice its texture, weight, shape, and temperature. Run your fingers over it and truly feel its presence.

4. **Engage Your Senses**: Pay attention to any physical sensations the object brings. Is it warm or cool to the touch? Does it have any interesting features or patterns? The goal is to stay focused on the object and away from the racing thoughts in your mind.

5. **Breathe and Relax**: While focusing on the object, continue to breathe slowly and deeply. Allow each breath to bring you back to the present moment, calming your mind and body with every exhale.

6. **Stay with It**: Continue focusing on the object for a few minutes. When your mind starts to wander, gently bring your focus back to the object, and continue to engage your senses.

Tracking Your Grounding Practice

What to Notice:

- Your stress level before and after grounding (1-10 scale)
- How your focus shifted from anxiety or stress to the present moment
- The physical sensations you experienced with the object
- Whether grounding helped improve emotional clarity or reduce anxiety
- How long it took for you to feel calmer and more balanced

Grounding Object Log:

Date: ________ **Time:** ________ **Location:** ________________

Duration: ________

Stress Level Before: 1-10______________

Stress Level After: 1-10________________

Object Used: ____

What I noticed: ☐ Felt more grounded ☐ Felt calmer ☐ Felt more focused ☐ Reduced anxiety ☐ Improved emotional clarity

Best part of this session: ______________________________

What I'd change next time: ______________________________

Will I use this technique again? ☐ Definitely ☐ Maybe ☐ Probably not

Weekly Reflection:

After practicing for a week, what patterns do you notice? How has grounding with an object impacted your stress levels, emotional balance, and overall well-being? Are there specific objects that work better for you in calming your mind?

27

Light a Candle

Your Simple Path to Tranquility

There's something about candlelight that instantly transforms a room, turning it from ordinary to peaceful. Whether it's the warm flicker of the flame or the gentle scent that fills the air, lighting a candle can create the perfect ambiance for relaxation. In this chapter, we'll explore how the simple act of lighting a candle can help you unwind, soothe your mind, and foster a calming atmosphere.

Candle lighting isn't just a way to brighten a room, it's a way to enhance your emotional well-being. The soft glow and fragrance can help you de-stress, clear your mind, and create a peaceful environment that promotes relaxation. It's a small ritual that can have a big impact on your mood and stress levels.

Why Lighting a Candle Works: The Power of Soft Light and Scent

Lighting a candle is more than just a physical action, it's an invitation to slow down and focus on the present moment. The warm, flickering light creates a calming effect on your nervous system, helping to lower heart rate and reduce stress. Additionally, many candles are infused with essential oils that can promote relaxation and improve mood. Scents like lavender, chamomile, or sandalwood have been shown to decrease anxiety and enhance feelings of peace and tranquility. The act of focusing on the gentle flame can also help quiet your mind, giving you a break from mental clutter and offering a moment of stillness.

Step-by-Step: How to Light a Candle for Relaxation

Let's dig into how you can use candlelight to create a calming environment:

1. **Choose Your Candle**: Pick a candle that appeals to your senses. Whether it's a favorite scent or a simple unscented candle, choose one that feels comforting. If you're using a scented candle, select a fragrance known for its relaxing properties, like lavender or eucalyptus.

2. **Find a Quiet Space**: Sit or lie down in a comfortable place where you can focus on the candle. This could be a cozy corner, your bedroom, or even a space near a window where you can enjoy the soft glow.

3. **Light the Candle**: Slowly light the wick and watch the flame begin to flicker. Take a deep breath, and allow yourself to pause. Focus on the warmth and the gentle movement of the flame.

4. **Focus on the Flame**: As the candle burns, focus on the flame and its calming movement. Let your mind become absorbed in the soft glow, and allow any tension in your body to melt away with each breath.

5. **Breathe and Relax**: Take deep, slow breaths as you continue to gaze at the candle. With each inhale, imagine yourself drawing in calmness and peace, and with each exhale, release any stress or anx-

iety.

6. **Sit in Stillness**: Stay with the candle for at least 5-10 minutes. There's no rush. Simply enjoy the moment of stillness and the soothing effect the candle provides.

Tracking Your Candle Lighting Practice

What to Notice:

- Your stress level before and after lighting the candle (1-10 scale)
- How your mood shifted after focusing on the candle
- Whether the light and scent helped you feel calmer and more relaxed
- Any changes in physical sensations (e.g., relaxation in your body, slower breathing)
- The best times of day to light a candle for relaxation

Candle Lighting Log:

Date: _________ **Time:** _________ **Location:** ____________________

Duration: _________

Stress Level Before: 1-10___________________

Stress Level After: 1-10____________________

Scent (if applicable): ____

What I noticed: ☐ Felt more relaxed ☐ Mood improved ☐ Felt calmer ☐ Enjoyed the peaceful ambiance ☐ Reduced anxiety

Best part of this session: ________________________________

What I'd change next time: ________________________________

Will I use this technique again? ☐ Definitely ☐ Maybe ☐ Probably not

Weekly Reflection:

After practicing for a week, what patterns do you notice? How has lighting a candle impacted your stress levels and mood? Are there certain scents or times of day that work best for creating a calming atmosphere?

28

Do a One-Minute Task

Your Instant Solution to Breaking Inertia

Have you ever found yourself stuck in a cycle of procrastination, unable to get started on anything? Sometimes, the hardest part is simply getting moving. But here's the secret: one-minute tasks. These small, simple actions are the perfect antidote to inertia, helping you break free from the feeling of being stuck and giving you that first burst of momentum. In this chapter, we'll explore how completing tiny tasks can boost your productivity, reduce stress, and help you regain focus.

It doesn't matter how big or small the task is, the key is to start. Whether it's making your bed, responding to an email, or putting away a single dish, taking just one minute to complete something can create a feeling of accomplishment and get your energy flowing. Once you start, you'll often find that momentum builds, and suddenly, you're ready to take on more.

Why One-Minute Tasks Work: The Power of Small Wins

One-minute tasks are effective because they are small enough to avoid overwhelm, but they still provide the satisfaction of crossing something off your to-do list. When you complete a quick task, it releases dopamine, the "*feel-good*" chemical in your brain, which boosts motivation and makes you want to keep going. It's like giving yourself a mini reward for just showing up, and it sets the stage for bigger accomplishments.

These short tasks help create a sense of progress and control. When we feel productive, even in small ways, it reduces stress and encourages a positive mindset. Instead of getting bogged down by everything you haven't done, focusing on one simple task can bring clarity and a feeling of calm.

Step-by-Step: How to Tackle a One-Minute Task

Let's take a look at how you can use one-minute tasks to create momentum:

1. **Choose a Simple Task**: Pick something small and manageable that you can complete in one minute. It could be something like making your bed, organizing a single drawer, or tidying up your desk.

2. **Set a Timer**: Set a timer for one minute to keep it short and focused. This helps prevent any distractions and adds a sense of urgency to get the task done.

3. **Focus and Complete the Task**: Start the task and give it your full attention. Complete it within the minute. The goal is to focus entirely on this one thing, without multitasking or overthinking.

4. **Celebrate the Small Win**: Once the task is complete, take a moment to appreciate the sense of accomplishment. This small action will give you a quick boost and help set a positive tone for the rest of your day.

5. **Repeat When Needed**: If you're feeling stuck again, tackle another one-minute task. The more you complete, the more momentum you'll gain, and soon, you'll be ready to take on bigger tasks.

Tracking Your One-Minute Task Practice

What to Notice:

- Your stress level before and after completing the task (1-10 scale)
- How completing the task impacted your mood and energy
- Whether you felt more focused or motivated to do other tasks afterward
- The types of tasks that made you feel most accomplished or satisfied
- The best times of day to incorporate one-minute tasks

One-Minute Task Log:

Date: _________ **Time**: _________ **Location**: _________________

Duration: _________

Stress Level Before: 1-10___________

Stress Level After: 1-10_____________

Task Completed: ____

What I noticed: ¨ ☐Felt more focused ¨ ☐Energy increased ¨ ☐Mood improved ¨ ☐Felt accomplished ¨ ☐Reduced stress

Best part of this session: ________________________________

What I'd change next time: ________________________________

Will I use this technique again? ☐ Definitely ☐ Maybe ☐ Probably not

Weekly Reflection:
After practicing for a week, what patterns do you notice? How have one-minute tasks impacted your stress levels, productivity, and focus? Which small tasks have been most effective in giving you momentum?

Conclusion: Your Journey to Lasting Well-Being

Congratulations! You've now explored 28 powerful techniques for managing stress and enhancing your emotional well-being. From the foundational practice of box breathing to the simple joy of lighting a candle, each step in this journey has been designed to give you practical, accessible tools that can transform how you respond to life's challenges.

The Power of Small Steps

Throughout this book, we've emphasized one crucial truth: small, consistent actions create profound change. You don't need hours of meditation or expensive equipment to experience relief from stress. Sometimes, the most powerful moments of healing come from taking five minutes to stretch, writing down three things you're grateful for, or simply drinking a glass of water mindfully.

The beauty of these 28 techniques lies not just in their simplicity, but in their flexibility. Your stress relief toolkit is now filled with options that can fit into any schedule, any budget, and any lifestyle. Whether you're at your desk feeling overwhelmed, lying in bed unable to sleep, or walking through a difficult period in your life, you have strategies at your fingertips.

Building Your Personal Practice

As you move forward, remember that there's no "*perfect*" way to use these techniques. Some days you might find yourself drawn to the physical practices like stretching or taking a warm bath. Other days, your mind might crave the clarity that comes from journaling or doing a brain dump. Listen to your body and honor what you need in each moment.

Consider creating your own personalized stress relief menu by identifying which techniques resonate most strongly with you. Perhaps box breathing becomes your go-to morning practice, while a gratitude list bookends your evening. Maybe you discover that combining techniques, like listening to calming music while sipping herbal tea—amplifies their benefits.

The Ripple Effect of Self-Care

As you integrate these practices into your daily life, you'll likely notice something wonderful happening: the benefits extend far beyond stress relief. When you take time to care for your emotional well-being, you become more present with loved ones, more creative in problem-solving, and more resilient in the face of challenges. Your commitment to self-care gives others permission to do the same. By modeling healthy stress management, you contribute to a culture where taking care of mental health is normalized and celebrated. This is one of the most generous gifts you can offer both yourself and those around you.

Embracing Progress Over Perfection

Remember that building new habits takes time, and that's perfectly okay. Some techniques will feel natural immediately, while others might require more practice before they feel comfortable. Be patient with yourself as you explore what works best for your unique situation and personality. If you find yourself forgetting to use these techniques during stressful moments, don't worry; this is part of the learning process. Consider setting gentle reminders on your phone, placing visual cues in your environment, or asking a trusted friend to check in with you about your self-care practices.

Your Record Pages: A Proof of Growth

The record pages you've been filling out throughout this journey serve as more than just tracking tools, they're a proof of your commitment to growth and self-awareness. Take time to review these pages periodically. You'll likely be surprised by the patterns you discover and the progress you've made. These records also serve as a valuable resource during particularly challenging times. When stress feels overwhelming, you can look back at your notes to remember which techniques have helped you most in the past. Your own experiences become your most trusted guide.

Stress is an inevitable part of life, but suffering is optional. With these 28 techniques in your toolkit, you're equipped to meet whatever challenges come your way with greater calm, clarity, and confidence. You've learned that you have more control over your emotional state than you might have realized, and that control comes not from avoiding stress entirely, but from responding to it skillfully. As you continue on your journey, remember that self-care isn't selfish, it's essential. By taking care of your own emotional well-being, you ensure that you can show up fully for all the important people and purposes in your life. The path to emotional well-being isn't a destination you arrive at once and stay forever. It's an ongoing practice, a daily choice to prioritize your mental health and respond to stress with intention rather than reaction. Some days will be easier than others, and that's completely normal.

Your Invitation to Thrive

As we close this book together, I want to leave you with this invitation: give yourself permission to thrive. Give yourself permission to take breaks when you need them, to ask for help when you're struggling, and to celebrate the small victories along the way. You now have 28 different ways to return to center, to find calm in the storm, and to nurture your emotional well-being. Trust in these practices, trust in your ability to care for yourself, and trust in your resilience. Your journey to lasting well-being continues beyond these pages. Take with you the knowledge that within you lies an incredible capacity for healing, growth, and peace. You have everything you need to not just survive life's stresses, but to transform them into opportunities for greater wisdom, compassion, and strength.

The tools are in your hands. The choice is yours. The time is now. Here's to your continued journey toward emotional well-being and the vibrant, peaceful life you deserve.

-- Liz Sheridan

References

Balban, M. Y., Neri, E., Kogon, M. M., Weed, L., Nouriani, B., Jo, B., Holl, G., Zeitzer, J. M., Spiegel, D., & Huberman, A. D. (2023). Brief structured respiration practices enhance mood and reduce physiological arousal. *Cell Reports Medicine*, 4(1), 100895. https://doi.org/10.1016/j.xcrm.2022.100895

Basso, J. C., McHale, A., Ende, V., Oberlin, D. J., & Suzuki, W. A. (2019). Brief, daily meditation enhances attention, memory, mood, and emotional regulation in non-experienced meditators. *Behavioural Brain Research*, 356, 208-220. https://doi.org/10.1016/j.bbr.2018.08.023

Bratman, G. N., Hamilton, J. P., Hahn, K. S., Daily, G. C., & Gross, J. J. (2015). Nature experience reduces rumination and subgenual prefrontal cortex activation. *Proceedings of the National Academy of Sciences*, 112(28), 8567-8572. https://doi.org/10.1073/pnas.1510459112

Cheng, S. T., Tsui, P. K., & Lam, J. H. (2015). Improving mental health in health care practitioners: Randomized controlled trial of a gratitude intervention. *Journal of Consulting and Clinical Psychology*, 83(1), 177-186. https://doi.org/10.1037/a0037895

Emmons, R. A., & McCullough, M. E. (2003). Counting blessings versus burdens: An experimental investigation of gratitude and subjective well-being in daily life. *Journal of Personality and Social Psychology*, 84(2), 377-389. https://doi.org/10.1037/0022-3514.84.2.377

Fourianalistyawati, E., Uswatun, D. A., & Chairunnisa, A. (2020). The effectiveness of progressive muscle relaxation technique on stress among university students. *KnE Social Sciences*, 4(15), 82-92. https://doi.org/10.18502/kss.v4i15.8204

Goyal, M., Singh, S., Sibinga, E. M., Gould, N. F., Rowland, Seymour, A., Sharma, R., Berger, Z., Sleicher, D., Maron, D. D., Shihab, H. M.,

Ranasinghe, P. D., Linn, S., Saha, S., Bass, E. B., & Haythornthwaite, J. A. (2014). Meditation programs for psychological stress and well-being: A systematic review and meta-analysis. *JAMA Internal Medicine*, 174(3), 357-368. https://doi.org/10.1001/jamainternalmedicine.2013.13018

Jacka, F. N., O'Neil, A., Opie, R., Itsiopoulos, C., Cotton, S., Mohebbi, M., Castle, D., Dash, S., Mihalopoulos, C., Chatterton, M. L., Brazionis, L., Dean, O. M., Hodge, A. M., & Berk, M. (2017). A randomised controlled trial of dietary improvement for adults with major depression (the 'SMILES' trial). *BMC Medicine*, 15(1), 23. https://doi.org/10.1186/s12916-017-0791-y

Khoury, B., Sharma, M., Rush, S. E., & Fournier, C. (2015). Mindfulness-based stress reduction for healthy individuals: A meta-analysis. *Journal of Health Psychology*, 20(6), 725-735. https://doi.org/10.1177/1359105315569095

Kong, F., Wang, X., Hu, S., & Liu, J. (2015). Neural correlates of psychological resilience and their relation to life satisfaction in a sample of healthy young adults. *NeuroImage*, 123, 165-172. https://doi.org/10.1016/j.neuroimage.2015.08.020

Lambert, N. M., Fincham, F. D., & Stillman, T. F. (2012). Gratitude and depressive symptoms: The role of positive reframing and positive emotion. *Cognition & Emotion*, 26(4), 615-633. https://doi.org/10.1080/02699931.2011.595393

Lemay, V., Hoolahan, J., & Buchanan, A. (2019). Impact of a yoga and meditation intervention on students' stress and anxiety levels. *American Journal of Pharmaceutical Education*, 83(5), 747-752. https://doi.org/10.5688/ajpe7001

Li, Q., Morimoto, K., Kobayashi, M., Inagaki, H., Katsumata, M., Hirata, Y., Hirata, K., Suzuki, H., Li, Y., Wakayama, Y., Kawada, T., Park, B. J., Ohira, T., Matsui, N., Kagawa, T., Miyazaki, Y., & Krensky, A.

M. (2008). Visiting a forest, but not a city, increases human natural killer activity and expression of anti-cancer proteins. *International Journal of Immunopathology and Pharmacology*, 21(1), 117-127. https://doi.org/10.1177/039463200802100113

Ma, X., Yue, Z. Q., Gong, Z. Q., Zhang, H., Duan, N. Y., Shi, Y. T., Wei, G. X., & Li, Y. F. (2017). The effect of diaphragmatic breathing on attention, negative affect and stress in healthy adults. *Frontiers in Psychology*, 8, 874. https://doi.org/10.3389/fpsyg.2017.00874

Morgan, S. P., Lengacher, C. A., & Seo, Y. (2024). A systematic review of breathing exercise interventions: An integrative complementary approach for anxiety and stress in adult populations. *American Journal of Health Promotion*, 38(7), 945-958. https://doi.org/10.1177/08980101241273860

Olafsdottir, G., Cloke, P., Schulz, A., van Dyck, Z., Eysteinsson, T., Thorleifsdottir, B., & Vögele, C. (2020). Health benefits of walking in nature: A randomized controlled study under conditions of real-life stress. *Environment and Behavior*, 52(3), 248-274. https://doi.org/10.1177/0013916518800798

Pennebaker, J. W., & Beall, S. K. (1986). Confronting a traumatic event: Toward an understanding of inhibition and disease. *Journal of Abnormal Psychology*, 95(3), 274-281. https://doi.org/10.1037/0021-843X.95.3.274

Remskar, M., Lojen, A., Roskar, S., & Bevk, T. (2024). Mindfulness improves psychological health and supports health behaviour cognitions: Evidence from a pragmatic RCT of a digital mindfulness-based intervention. *British Journal of Health Psychology*, 29(3), 745-763. https://doi.org/10.1111/bjhp.12745

Riegel, B., Dunbar, S. B., Fitzsimons, D., Freedland, K. E., Lee, C. S., Middleton, S., Stromberg, A., Vellone, E., Webber, D. E., & Jaarsma, T. (2021). Self-care research: Where are we now? Where are we going? *International Journal of Nursing Studies*, 116, 103402. https://doi.

org/10.1016/j.ijnurstu.2019.103402

Sethi, S., Wingfield, B., McCormack, J., & Sanchez, H. (2023). Effectiveness of nature-based walking interventions in improving mental health in adults: A systematic review. *Current Psychology*, 43(8), 7234-7252. https://doi.org/10.1007/s12144-023-05112-z

Sood, A., Prasad, K., Schroeder, D., & Varkey, P. (2011). Stress management and resilience training among Department of Medicine faculty: A pilot randomized clinical trial. *Journal of General Internal Medicine*, 26(8), 858-861. https://doi.org/10.1007/s11606-011-1640-x

Thompson Coon, J., Boddy, K., Stein, K., Whear, R., Barton, J., & Depledge, M. H. (2011). Does participating in physical activity in outdoor natural environments have a greater effect on physical and mental wellbeing than physical activity indoors? A systematic review. *Environmental Science & Technology*, 45(5), 1761-1772. https://doi.org/10.1021/es102947t

van der Zwan, J. E., de Vente, W., Huizink, A. C., Bögels, S. M., & de Bruin, E. I. (2015). Physical activity, mindfulness meditation, or heart rate variability biofeedback for stress reduction: A randomized controlled trial. *Applied Psychology: Health and Well-Being*, 7(2), 230-248. https://doi.org/10.1111/aphw.12047

Watson, S. L., Weeks, B. K., Weis, L. J., Harding, A. T., Horan, S. A., & Beck, B. R. (2018). High-intensity resistance and impact training improves bone mineral density and physical function in postmenopausal women with osteoporosis or osteopenia: The LIFTMOR randomized controlled trial. *Journal of Bone and Mineral Research*, 33(2), 211-220. https://doi.org/10.1002/jbmr.3284

Yavuz Sercekman, M. (2024). Exploring the sustained impact of the Mindfulness-Based Stress Reduction program: A thematic analysis. *Frontiers in Psychology*, 15, 1347336. https://doi.org/10.3389/fpsyg.2024.1347336

Printed in Dunstable, United Kingdom

66095364R00097